Promoting Language and Early Literacy Development

Combining teaching experience, research findings, and first-hand parenting stories, this compelling and practical resource distils everything you need to know for a thorough understanding of language and early literacy development. Following the introductory chapter, each chapter focuses on a component of language and early literacy including oral language development, listening comprehension, vocabulary development, phonological and phonemic awareness, alphabet knowledge and phonics instruction, handwriting and writing conventions, morphological awareness, digital literacy skills, and motivation for literacy. With an emphasis on the diversity of classrooms and types of learners, *Promoting Language and Early Literacy Development: Practical Insights from a Parent Researcher* is invaluable reading for parents and caregivers, early years teachers, learning support assistants, and nursery workers.

Dr. Pamela Beach is an Associate Professor of Language and Literacy at the Faculty of Education at Queen's University in Kingston, Canada. Pamela completed her M.A. in Child Study and Education and her Ph.D. in Developmental Psychology and Education at the University of Toronto. Her background as a parent and elementary teacher has influenced her research interests which focus on the dissemination of research-informed literacy practices.

T0383689

Other Eye on Education Books
Available from Routledge
(www.routledge.com/eyeoneducation)

Literacy for All: A Framework for Anti-Oppressive Teaching
Shawna Coppola

**Early Literacy Matters: A Leader's Guide to
Systematic Change**
Carol E. Canady and Robert Lynn Canady

**Shifting the Balance, Grades K-2: 6 Ways to Bring the Science
of Reading into the Balanced Literacy Classroom**
Jan Burkins and Kari Yates

**Supporting Early Speech-Language Development:
Strategies for Ages 0-8**
Kimberly A. Boynton

**Empowering Young Children: How to Nourish Deep,
Transformative Learning for Social Justice**
Wendy Ostroff

**Promoting Language and Early Literacy Development:
Practical Insights from a Parent Researcher**
Pamela Beach

Promoting Language and Early Literacy Development

Practical Insights from a Parent Researcher

Pamela Beach

Routledge
Taylor & Francis Group

NEW YORK AND LONDON

Designed cover image: © Eli Campbell

First published 2025
by Routledge
605 Third Avenue, New York, NY 10158

and by Routledge
4 Park Square, Milton Park, Abingdon, Oxon, OX14 4RN

Routledge is an imprint of the Taylor & Francis Group, an informa business

ISBN: 978-1-032-68854-1 (hbk)
ISBN: 978-1-032-67323-3 (pbk)
ISBN: 978-1-032-68855-8 (ebk)

DOI: 10.4324/9781032688558

Typeset in Palatino
by SPi Technologies India Pvt Ltd (Straive)

For Eli

Contents

Acknowledgements

This book stems from short blog posts about language and early literacy development I began writing during my first sabbatical in 2022–23. At the time, my son Eli had just turned one and much of my inspiration to write came from him and his language and early literacy behaviours. I am extremely fortunate for the enormous amount of time I had to spend with Eli during this sabbatical.

Along with the inspiration that came from Eli, I was also fortunate to meet with and talk to teachers from early years and elementary schools. I am thankful for the insights these teachers shared with me and that I present throughout this book. Their passion for literacy and engaging the children they teach in literacy-rich activities are truly appreciated.

I also owe a debt of gratitude to my partner, Matt, who has ventured on the parent journey with me, and provided me with encouragement and a listening ear right from this book's inception.

Many thanks to John Kirby who provided me with valuable feedback on several chapters. I would also like to extend my thanks to Rebecca Luce-Kapler who was the first to encourage me to submit a book proposal based on my parent researcher perspective.

Thank you also to the team at Routledge, especially to Alexis O'Brien for her constant support.

Finally, my deepest thanks to my parents, Jane and Ross, who listened to my many musings about this book and Eli's language endeavours.

Meet the Author

Dr. Pamela Beach is an Associate Professor of Language and Literacy at the Faculty of Education at Queen's University in Kingston, Canada. Pamela completed her M.A. in Child Study and Education and her Ph.D. in Developmental Psychology and Education at the University of Toronto. Her background as a parent and elementary teacher has influenced her research interests which focus on the dissemination of research-informed literacy practices.

1

Turning Pages

An Introduction

When my son, Eli, turned one I took notice of the way he started interacting with his toys and communicating about his environment. His glances at objects seemed to have evolved to a point where he began eyeing familiar belongings and images in new ways—he seemed to be more observant, taking in new information from the world around him and wanting to share experiences with a nearby observer. I watched for these latest behaviours in different contexts and with different materials, including when Eli interacted with books from his board book collection (which had grown into a quite a library thanks to friends, family, and thrift stores). Eli had been turning the pages of these books for some time, as most babies do. But approaching his first birthday, he began stopping after each turn, glancing back and forth at each page laid out in front of him, perhaps seeing the eyes of an illustrated animal for the first time or noticing the strange symbols on each page (not realizing, of course, that these strange symbols were the letters of the alphabet). The books were usually right side up and Eli usually turned the pages from the front of the book to the back, although at the time he seemed just as engaged when the book was upside down. After turning a page, he would sometimes verbalize a single-syllable utterance and gesture or point to the picture while catching my eye, "telling"

DOI: 10.4324/9781032688558-1

me about what he noticed. Whether the book was held upright or turned from back to front, these were early print concepts and book handling skills developing, and over time, these print concepts would look more and more like reading. Reading (that is, reading at the word level and actually comprehending text) is a complex activity that involves decoding and language-related skills, but here I was seeing "reading" happen at a very basic level. Even if someone might argue that this was not really reading, there was still a connection being made about how this board book, with words and illustrations, was telling Eli something.

These pre-reading behaviours are built upon the development of oral language and early literacy skills. From learning a language, which is something that we are wired to do, to reading symbols of a particular language, a relatively recent invention (when you consider the existence of the human brain) and an activity that does not happen naturally, early language development has indeed been linked to later reading achievement (Shanahan & Lonigan, 2012).

I find it fascinating that infants are born ready to take up any language, and within about six to eight months it's already been decided which language or languages will be dominant (Hay et al., 2011). Up until about six to eight months, an infant can detect sounds in any language, a feat that adults cannot do. As infants hear their native language more and more, they begin to recognize sounds and combinations of sounds in the language that will become dominant. If you add up the sounds from all the world's languages, there are about 600 consonant speech sounds and 200 vowel speech sounds (Kirby, 2019). English uses 44 of these speech sounds, whereas Japanese, for example, uses 20, and Finnish uses 21. Infants who are surrounded by the sounds of the English language will eventually distinctly hear English's 24 consonant sounds and 20 vowel sounds (in Japanese, it would be 15 consonant sounds and 5 vowel sounds, and in Finnish, 13 consonant sounds and 8 vowel sounds). As infants detect the sounds in the language they hear most often, they begin to correctly articulate each sound or combination of sounds. This is a huge achievement in speech development and critically important to language learning and eventually to reading. From birth to around age seven, there's a *critical period* for learning a language, a time in which learning a language is especially susceptible to and even requires specific environmental influences (Purves et al., 2001). According to Patricia Kuhl, during the first period in language development infants are "linguistic geniuses" (Kuhl, 2011). In her research, Kuhl describes how babies begin life as "citizens of the world" ready to take on any language. As babies take in statistics on how frequently they hear sounds in their native and non-native languages, the language that will become dominant begins to narrow. They build a repertoire of speech sounds from the language that surrounds them and relatively quickly become "language-bound listeners" (Kuhl, 2011).

Maria Montessori, the founder of the Montessori approach, described the critical period for language and early literacy development (from birth to about age eight) as a space in which a child's interests are focused on developing a certain skill (Montessori, 1995). During a child's preschool years (approximately 18 to 34 months), for instance, Montessori believed that children are drawn to language and words like moths to a flame, and are particularly excited about identifying objects, rhyming words, and repeating words (Montessori, 1995). According to Montessori, supporting children during the sensitive period for language means telling oral stories, naming objects around us, using real words for things, singing songs, reading poems and books aloud, and having rich conversations throughout the day (Multilingual Montessori, 2023). Supporting children's language and early literacy skills starts with these types of oral games and dialogues. Long before children enter school, their language skills go through major milestones building a foundation for learning to read.

I've included Maria Montessori's perspective here as an introduction of what's to come in the remaining chapters of this book, particularly in relation to conversations I've had with Montessori teachers about their language and literacy perceptions and practices. I've been interested in language and early literacy development for some time now, as an elementary teacher, as a parent, and especially in my research over the past several years talking to teachers about how they teach literacy and where they find information and resources to contribute to and enrich their literacy programmes. I've always found that the teachers I talk to, regardless of the grade or type of school, teach with passion and ensure that they are supporting all their students by looking for information that is research-informed and directly related to their students' needs (e.g., Beach et al., 2021; Beach et al., 2020). Throughout this book, my aim is to highlight aspects of the conversations I've had with teachers about their perceptions and practices of language and early literacy based on conversations from a study I conducted in 2022–23. I will also detail practices from my own professional experience as an elementary teacher, and as the introduction of this chapter implies, I will share some of my son's feats in language and early literacy development. My intention of this book is twofold: to outline what the research says about language and early literacy skills, and to share research-based activities that parents and teachers can do to foster language and literacy development at home and in the classroom.

Parents are indeed their child's first teacher. Even if a parent isn't explicitly thinking about what to teach and how to teach it, their everyday interactions with their infant, toddler, or pre-schooler foster language and early literacy learning and development. Whether it's pointing out a sign on the way to daycare, reciting a favourite rhyme, or cuddling up with a picture book, parent–child interactions that involve oral language and print set the foundation for early literacy skills and eventually reading. Research has provided evidence that home literacy learning, prior to a child entering school, is associated with later reading skills, including letter knowledge at age five and word reading skills in grades one and two (Hood et al., 2008), vocabulary growth in kindergarten and grade one (Sénéchal & LeFevre, 2002), and reading comprehension in grades two and three (Inoue et al., 2018). Each chapter will discuss these and other language and literacy topics in detail and highlight ways in which parents can incorporate games and activities into their everyday interactions with their child. Along with parents, this book is geared towards early years and primary teachers new to the world of language and early literacy. Skills that can be fostered in the classroom will be highlighted in each chapter and practical classroom activities will be shared.

Before delving into Chapter 2's discussion of oral language development, I'll briefly describe the study I conducted in 2022–23. I'll also discuss two theoretical frameworks related to language and literacy development. The first is *the simple view of reading*, which shows the relationship between language, print, and the complexities of reading (Hoover & Gough, 1990). The second framework stems from the work of Linnea Ehri, an educational psychologist and expert on reading development. Ehri proposed a four-phase model to help delineate a child's growth in learning to read words (1999; 2023). Each of these frameworks sets a foundation for understanding the link between language, literacy development, and reading, and aspects of each will be discussed in relation to the chapter topics throughout the book.

The research study

In 2022–23, I was fortunate to visit several early years and elementary schools and talk to early years and primary teachers about how they perceive and practise language and early literacy education (Beach, 2024). Seven of the teachers I spoke to were Montessori teachers from three countries—Canada, Mexico, and Italy—and five teachers were from three different independent schools across two provinces in Canada. Most of the conversations occurred after I toured the teacher's school or following an observation in which I had the opportunity to watch a teacher and her students engage in a literacy-related experience. All the conversations began with general questions about the teachers' background experiences and evolved into discussions about their language and literacy perceptions and practices, including how they defined literacy, their literacy programmes and assessments, and resources they used to support their professional learning in literacy education. I found that the teachers across the three countries and types of schools held similar beliefs about the foundational components of literacy. For instance, all the teachers

I met with talked about the critical importance of oral language development and supporting children's understanding of spoken language and effective communication; oral language was foundational to their literacy programme. I was excited, but not surprised, by the fact that the teachers' perceptions aligned with what the research says about effective language and early literacy development and instruction; researchers generally agree that early literacy involves developing oral language, vocabulary, listening comprehension, and phonological and morphological awareness, as well as decoding skills, print awareness, letter knowledge, and early skills in writing (Lonigan & Shanahan, 2009; Rand & Morrow, 2021; Snow, 2017). I recognize that this is a small sample of teachers and that their narratives are context-specific; however, it is my hope that the insights they shared with me and that I present throughout this book can provide you, the reader, with additional practical examples of language and literacy learning experiences. You can find instances from the study in most chapters under the heading *from the field*.

The simple view of reading

Earlier in this chapter I described how reading symbols of a particular language is a relatively recent invention. Reading is also an activity that does not happen naturally but requires systematic and explicit instruction in various print and language-related skills (Snow, 2017). Consider *the simple view of reading* (Figure 1.1) which shows how reading comprehension (understanding written text) is a product of decoding or print-related skills and linguistic comprehension or language-related skills (Hoover & Gough, 1990).

Decoding skills are those that promote the ability to recognize and read words, while language-related skills are those that support the ability to make meaning of text. According to

FIGURE 1.1 The simple view of reading.

the simple view of reading, both sets of skills contribute to reading comprehension. If someone can easily decode print but has weaknesses in vocabulary or background knowledge, or syntax and grammar (components of linguistic comprehension), they will have difficulty applying any meaning to the words they are reading. Likewise, if someone has trouble decoding words, even though they have strong language-related skills, they too will have difficulties comprehending text.

The simple view of reading has been used by researchers and educators for several decades to provide a relatively straightforward way of understanding the complexities of reading. It highlights the fact that successful readers need to do more than just sound out words and has been consistently supported by research showing that to extract meaning from text (to become a good comprehender), an individual must develop skills in both decoding and language (e.g., Lonigan & Shanahan, 2009; Rand & Morrow, 2021). Decoding or print-related skills include concepts of print, alphabet knowledge, letter-sound associations, and the application of phonemic awareness, whereas linguistic comprehension or language-related skills include phonology, vocabulary, morphology, background knowledge, syntax, and semantics.

A language-rich environment right from birth can provide opportunities for "talk," enriching vocabulary and leading to early language and literacy skills, like phonological awareness and alphabet knowledge which, as *the simple view of reading* shows, are directly connected to learning to read. When babies and toddlers are surrounded by books and these books are read to them often, they begin opening books on their own, and like Eli, they start noticing what's on the page. With supports and materials, toddlers and preschoolers begin to develop an awareness of how print works and that what's on the page conveys a message to the reader.

Phases of reading development

Ehri's framework for understanding reading development includes four phases: pre-alphabetic, partial alphabetic, full alphabetic, and consolidated alphabetic (see Figure 1.2). Each phase outlines the

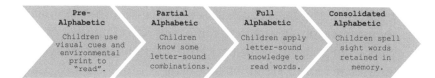

FIGURE 1.2 Ehri's phases of reading development.

process of learning to read English words and aligns with approximate ages; although as I note below, Ehri's model is meant to be flexible in terms of each phase's associated age and grade level, as well as with respect to the sequence in which an individual might progress. Some children do not necessarily progress through the four phases in a strict sequence. Ehri describes the process of learning to read as a *connection-forming* one, in which connections are formed in an individual's lexical memory (word bank) that link the written forms of the word to each word's pronunciation and meaning (1999, 2023).

At the earliest phase, the *pre-alphabetic phase*, children form connections between selected visual attributes of words and their pronunciations or meanings and store these associations in memory (Ehri, 2023). Cues that are associated with words occur separately from a child's ability to understand the letter-sound relationships. A child might, for instance, notice that the double -oo in *look*, looks like two eyes. This visual cue, in turn, might help a child to recognize that this word does in fact say *look*. Another example of children remembering the visual cues accompanying print rather than the written words themselves is a stop sign; the red octagon is associated with the word *stop*. This is *environmental print* where the name appears in a visual cue—road signs, food labels, and various brand logos, like McDonald's golden arches or Nike's swoosh are all examples of environmental print. It's the type of print that occurs in everyday life, and when referred to or pointed out, it's the contextual cues (not necessarily the letters) that become stored in memory as representative of a particular word (Ehri, 2005).

The next phase of Ehri's framework is the *partial alphabetic phase*. During this phase, children develop partial alphabetic connections between some of the letters in written words and sounds detected in their pronunciations (Ehri, 2023). This is likely to begin when a teacher or parent is systematically intro-ducing letter-sounds. For instance, an example of the first set of letter-sounds that a teacher might include in their scope and sequence is *a, m, s, t, p, f, i*, and *n* (UFLI, n.d.). These letters have been selected due to the relatively easy mouth formation that it takes to articulate each letter-sound (more on all things sound-related in Chapter 5). Children at this phase begin to read some words, based on the letter-sounds they have learned, and they also might use their beginning knowledge of letter-sound associa-tions to spell words, although more likely invent partial spellings of words by writing out the most salient sounds and leaving out other sounds, likely those sounds found in the middle of words. A child at this second phase in word learning might write the word *letter*, for instance, as *letr*. Inventive spelling can be a good mea-sure of informal assessment with respect to a child's phonemic awareness (their understanding that spoken words are composed of individual sounds), but more on this later in Chapter 5.

In the next phase of Ehri's framework, the *full alphabetic phase*, children have developed a full understanding that letters sym-bolize sounds, and they apply this understanding to read words more accurately (2023). Children who are explicitly taught the alphabetic code have the tools for decoding unfamiliar spellings of words by blending the sounds together. As children come across words they've learned more and more often, these words are eventually stored in memory and can be read automatically by sight. Ehri describes this process as *unitization*, where spell-ings of sight words are fully bonded to their pronunciations in memory (2023). Unitizing full words and reading these words with increased automaticity leads to children's ability to read more fluently, with automaticity, phrasing, and expression.

Finally, in the fourth phase known as the *consolidated alpha-betic phase*, children have developed the ability to retain complete information about the spellings of sight words in memory. This makes it possible for their print lexicons (the vocabulary or total number of words that a person knows) to rapidly grow (Ehri, 2023). As more and more words are retained in memory, letter patterns that recur across different words become consolidated. Eventually, readers can access words they've learned in memory and automatically read words. As children automatically recognize more and more words by sight and read with fluency, phrasing, and expressing, they can use their cognitive energy to make sense of what they are reading. Energy that would otherwise be spent on decoding words that are unfamiliar is used for comprehending text.

Ehri's framework for understanding reading development is meant to be flexible in terms of each phase's associated age and grade level, as well as with respect to the sequence in which an individual might progress. This framework, like *the simple view of reading*, can help parents understand the approximate skills involved in their child's language and early literacy development. Indeed, the pre-alphabetic phase isn't likely to occur until a toddler is around the age of two, but Ehri's framework does provide a sense of where a one-year-old might be headed in terms of their early literacy development. Educators can also use either of the two frameworks to better understand the range of skills that exist in the classroom. Additionally, these frameworks can contribute to the understanding of how children progress in learning to read words and help parents and teachers select appropriate strategies to support their children's early literacy and word reading skills.

The book's roadmap

Nine chapters follow this introductory chapter, each outlining a specific language and literacy-related skill. Chapter 2, *Linguistic Geniuses: Oral Language and Listening Comprehension*, continues the discussion of oral language development and the major feats that infants, toddlers, and children achieve. Topics include early and later language acquisition, milestones in early vocal and speech development, infant speech perception, receptive and expressive language, and supporting language development and listening comprehension through a language-rich environment. The chapter ends with a discussion of how parents and educators can foster oral language development at home and in the classroom.

Chapter 3, *Becoming Word Conscious: Vocabulary Development*, discusses how vocabulary develops, specifically meaning vocabulary, and how educators and parents can foster vocabulary development from an early age. Topics include early vocabulary acquisition, vocabulary and word knowledge, what it means to know a word (vocabulary depth and breadth), tiered vocabulary instruction, vocabulary and reading comprehension, and word consciousness.

Chapter 4, *Fostering Word Scientists: Language Syntax and Morphology*, delves into the topics syntax and morphology, and how grammar and word knowledge develop from a young age. A discussion of syntax and morphology and how both relate to reading is included in Chapter 4. Additional topics include grammar development and how children learn to use language correctly, etymology and its relation to morphology, as well as tips and tools for fostering the development of syntax and morphological awareness at home and in the classroom.

Chapter 5, *The Sounds of Language: Phonological and Phonemic Awareness*, covers the broad topics of phonological and phonemic awareness. Clear distinctions between these two constructs are discussed, as well as how they are related. Developmental progressions of phonological and phonemic awareness as well as examples of how to foster phonological and phonemic awareness at home and in the early primary grades are described.

In Chapter 6, *"The Cat Sat": Alphabet Knowledge and Phonics*, the discussion turns to print-related skills, including alphabet knowledge and phonics. Effective phonics instruction, the general sequence of phonics instruction, and the relation between phonics and reading, as well as between phonics and phonemic awareness, are discussed. Games and activities that can be implemented at home and in the classroom are also shared.

Chapter 7, *Meaning Makers: Reading Fluency and Comprehension*, shares instructional approaches to reading fluency and comprehension and how parents at home and teachers in the classroom can support their children in reading words automatically and making meaning from text. Topics include the key elements of reading fluency and strategic reading, the importance of prior knowledge for understanding text, making inferences, as well as additional scaffolds for supporting fluency and comprehension.

Chapter 8, *Mark Making: Letter Formation and Writing Development*, discusses how handwriting and the elements of writing develop. Topics that will be covered in Chapter 8 include letter formation and stages of handwriting, pencil grip and tips for helping children strengthen their fine motor skills, various approaches to teaching handwriting, and ways in which the elements of writing can be taught at home and in the classroom.

Chapter 9, *Interacting with Technologies: Developing Digital Literacy Skills*, discusses new literacies and the development of digital literacy skills. While there are concerns about screentime, especially in the early years, new literacies skills, including digital literacies, require attention across age groups. Topics address developmentally appropriate approaches to learning from and with technology and how concepts about print have evolved to now include concepts about different forms of text and media. This chapter emphasizes how to foster children's digital literacy skills from a critical standpoint.

Finally, Chapter 10, *Reading in Cars: Motivation for Literacy*, highlights how motivation for literacy sets a foundation for literacy and reading development, and discusses how self-efficacy, literacy engagement, support, choice, and time all impact motivation for literacy. Additional topics include intrinsic interest, self-concept and autonomy, and the link between motivation for literacy and reading.

Each chapter ends with a list of tips for parents and teachers to consider when supporting their child's or students' language and early literacy development. A second list of children's books is also included at the end of each chapter. These are books I recommend reading with your child or students when thinking about each chapter topic. These books can be thought of as *mentor texts* and can provide examples of reading structures and skills. Throughout the book, I use the term *early literacy* to include literacy-related skills that develop between 0 and about 8 years of age. Many researchers also use the term *emergent literacy* to denote skills that occur before a child begins reading on their own. I've chosen to consider *early literacy* as including skills that might fall under both emergent and early literacy, similar to how the National Early Literacy Panel described *early literacy* in their report on developing early literacy (Lonigan & Shanahan, 2009).

As the reader, you may decide to read this book from cover to cover; however, you are also invited to jump right into a chapter of interest. If, for instance, you are a grade one teacher interested in knowing more about phonics instruction—what phonics is and how to teach it—then you might decide to jump ahead to Chapter 6, which discusses all things related to alphabet knowledge and phonics. Similarly, if you are a parent interested in supporting your preschooler with activities in letter formation, you may be keen to go directly to Chapter 8, which shares information on mark making and writing development. Each chapter can stand on its own or be read sequentially, it is up to you to decide on the route you will take.

References

Beach, P. (2024). *Literacy perspectives and practices: Patterns across three countries. Annual conference of the Canadian Society for Studies in Education*, Montreal, Quebec.

Beach, P., Favret, E., & Minuk, A. (2021). Exploring teachers' cognitive processes and web-based actions during a series of self-directed online learning sessions. *International Journal of E-Learning & Distance Education Revue Internationale Du E-Learning Et La Formation à Distance*, *36*(1). https://www.ijede.ca/index.php/jde/article/view/1191

Beach, P., Henderson, G., & McConnel, J. (2020). Elementary teachers' cognitive processes and metacognitive strategies during self-directed online learning. *Teachers and Teaching*, *26*(5–6), 395–413. doi:10.1080/13540602.2020.1863206

Ehri, L.C. (2023). Phases of development in learning to read and spell words. *American Educator*, *47*(3), 17–18. https://files.eric.ed.gov/fulltext/EJ1394529.pdf

Ehri, L. C. (2005). Learning to read words: Theory, findings, and issues. *Scientific Studies of Reading*, *9*(2), 167–188.

Ehri, L.C. (1999). Phases of development in learning to read words. In: J. Oakhill & R. Beard (Eds.), *Reading development and the teaching of reading: A psychological perspective* (pp. 79–108). Blackwell Science.

Hay, J.F., Pelucchi, B., Estes, K.G., & Saffran, J.R. (2011). Linking sounds to meanings. Infant statistical learning in a natural language. *Cognitive Psychology, 63*(2), 93–106.

Hood, M., Conlon, E., & Andrews, G. (2008). Preschool home literacy practices and children's literacy development: A longitudinal analysis. *Journal of Educational Psychology, 100,* 252–271. doi:10.1037/0022-0663.100.2.252

Hoover, W.A., & Gough, P.B. (1990). The simple view of reading. *Reading and Writing, 2,* 127–160.

Inoue, T., Georgiou, G., Parrila, R., & Kirby, J.R. (2018). Examining an extended home literacy model: The mediating roles of emergent literacy skills and reading fluency. *Scientific Studies of Reading, 22*(4), 273–288. doi:10.1080/10888438.2018.1435663

Kirby, J.R. (2019). Word knowledge quality and literacy. In: J. Orrell & H. Askell-Williams (Eds.), *Problem solving for teaching and learning: A festschrift in honour of Emeritus Professor Mike Lawson* (pp. 48–66). New York: Routledge.

Kuhl, P.K. (2011). Social mechanisms in early language acquisition: Understanding integrated brain systems supporting language. In: J. Decety & J.T. Cacioppo (Eds.), *The Oxford handbook of social neuroscience* (pp. 649–667). Oxford University Press.

Lonigan, C.J., & Shanahan, T. (2009). *Executive summary: Developing early literacy: Report of the National Early Literacy Panel.* Washington, DC: National Institute for Literacy. https://files.eric.ed.gov/fulltext/ED508381.pdf

Montessori, M. (1995). *The absorbent mind.* Holt Paperbacks.

Multilingual Montessori. (2023). *Montessori resources and inspiration for raising multilingual children.* https://multilingualmontessori.org/

Purves, D., Augustine, G.J., Fitzpatrick, D., et al. (2001). *Neuroscience.* (2nd ed.). Sinauer Associates. https://www.ncbi.nlm.nih.gov/books/NBK11020/

Rand, M.K., & Morrow, L.M. (2021). The contribution of play experiences in early literacy: Expanding the science of reading. *Reading Research Quarterly, 56*(S1), S239–S248. https://doi.org/10.1002/rrq.383

Sénéchal, M., & LeFevre, J.-A. (2002). Parental involvement in the development of children's reading skill: A five-year longitudinal study. *Child Development*, *73*, 445–460. doi:10.1111/1467-8624.00417

Shanahan, T., & Lonigan, C. (2012). The role of early oral language in literacy development. *Language Magazine*, *12*(2), 24. https://www.languagemagazine.com/5100-2/

Snow, C.E. (2017). Early literacy development and instruction: An overview. In: N. Kucirkova, C.E. Snow, V. Grøver, & C. McBride-Chang (Eds.), *The Routledge international handbook of early literacy education: A contemporary guide to literacy teaching and interventions in a global context* (pp. 5–13). Routledge.

UFLI (University of Florida Literacy Institute). (n.d.). UFLI foundations. https://ufli.education.ufl.edu/foundations/

2

Linguistic Geniuses

Oral Language and Listening Comprehension

It seems like it was just yesterday that two-month-old Eli was communicating through coos and babbles. These early vocalizations would have slight variations depending on Eli's mood and whether he was hungry or tired, but they were indeed early forms of communication; attempts at trying to tell me or my partner something, even if these attempts were more instinctive than intentional. These early productions of sound seemed to turn into short phrases and sentences relatively quickly, as well as attempts at repeating every new word that came across Eli's radar. Over the course of just two years, like most babies and toddlers, Eli's ability to understand and respond to language started to reflect adult-like speech, incorporating the core facets of oral language—phonology, syntax, morphology, vocabulary, and semantics. I'll delve into each of these topics in subsequent chapters, but here in Chapter 2, I'll begin with a discussion of the phonological component of oral language in relation to the acquisition and development of speech sounds.

DOI: 10.4324/9781032688558-2

Milestones for speech and language development

Table 2.1 outlines the typical milestones for speech and language development (American Speech-Language-Hearing Association [ASHA], 2024). Along with those adorable coos and babbles, infants from birth to three months begin showing early signs of communication, like smiling in response to a change in a parent

TABLE 2.1 Milestones for speech and language development

Birth to 3 Months
◆ Alerts to loud sounds. ◆ Quiets or smiles when you talk. ◆ Makes sounds back and forth with you. ◆ Makes sounds that differ depending on whether they are happy or upset. ◆ Coos, makes sounds like **ooooo, aahh, and mmmmm**. ◆ Recognizes loved ones and some common objects. ◆ Turns or looks toward voices or people talking.
4 to 6 Months
◆ Giggles and laughs. ◆ Responds to facial expressions. ◆ Looks at objects of interest and follows objects with their eyes. ◆ Reacts to toys that make sounds, like those with bells or music. ◆ Vocalizes during play or with objects in mouth. ◆ Vocalizes different vowel sounds—sometimes combined with a consonant—like **uuuuuummm, aaaaaaagoo**, or **daaaaaaaaaa**. ◆ Blows "raspberries."
7 to 9 Months
◆ Looks at you when you call their name. ◆ Stops for a moment when you say, "No." ◆ Babbles long strings of sounds, like **mamamama, upup**, or **bababab**. ◆ Looks for loved ones when upset. ◆ Raises arms to be picked up. ◆ Recognizes the names of some people and objects. ◆ Pushes away unwanted objects.
10 to 12 Months
◆ By age 10 months, reaches for objects. ◆ Points, waves, and shows or gives objects. ◆ Imitates and initiates gestures for engaging in social interactions and playing games, like blowing kisses or playing peek-a-boo. ◆ Tries to copy sounds that you make. ◆ Enjoys dancing. ◆ Responds to simple words and phrases like "Go bye-bye" and "Look at Mommy." ◆ Says one or two-words-like mama, dada, hi, and bye.

(Continued)

TABLE 2.1 (Continued)

13 to 18 Months
◆ Looks around when asked "where" questions—like "Where's your blanket?" ◆ Follows directions—like "Give me the ball," "Hug the teddy bear," "Come here," or "Show me your nose." ◆ Points to make requests, to comment, or to get information. ◆ Shakes head for "no" and nods head for "yes." ◆ Understands and uses words for common objects, some actions, and people in their lives. ◆ Identifies one or more body parts. ◆ Uses gestures when excited, like clapping or giving a high-five, or when being silly, like sticking out their tongue or making funny faces. ◆ Uses a combination of long strings of sounds, syllables, and real words with speech-like inflection.
19 to 24 Months
◆ Uses and understands at least 50 different words for food, toys, animals, and body parts. Speech may not always be clear—like **du** for "shoe" or **dah** for "dog." ◆ Puts two or more words together—like **more water** or **go outside**. ◆ Follows two-step directions—like "Get the spoon and put it on the table." ◆ Uses words like **me, mine**, and **you**. ◆ Uses words to ask for help. ◆ Uses possessives, like **Daddy's sock**.

or caregiver's voice, and of course, crying, which is indeed a basic form of communication and can sound different depending on an infant's needs; an infant's cry to signify hunger is usually lower in pitch and often accompanied with a sucking motion with their mouth, whereas a cry to signify fatigue might sound nasally and increase in intensity (National Institute on Deafness and Other Communication Disorders [NIDCD], 2022). The earliest sounds infants produce are called *reflexive sounds*, which, as the term *reflexive* implies, are involuntary (Kuhl & Meltzoff, 1996). While an infant automatically produces these first sounds without intent, they can elicit a response from a nearby parent or caregiver (a parent might ask their two-month-old infant if they are okay or need to be held). Infants interact with their parents and caregivers through these types of sounds and additional gestures and movements. By the time an infant is nine or ten months, their interactions and responses become increasingly complex, and their sounds and gestures might turn into familiar games, like peek-a-boo and pat-a-cake (Kuhl & Meltzoff, 1996).

The milestones that an infant achieves in just the first year of life are incredible. For us adults, we might take some of these milestones for granted, not really stopping to consider how certain sounds and gestures are indeed indicative of language development. Laughing, for instance, usually begins around four to six months and is an important part of language learning (ASHA, 2024). It's the emotional tone of laughing that fosters social interactions and influences communication skills and language development.

I remember when Eli first, sort of, laughed. He was looking up at me from his crib and responding to something I was saying in my "motherese" voice, an infant-directed type of speech that's usually at a higher pitch than normal, slower, and consists of shorter sentences (Pence Turnbull & Justice, 2017). I remember looking down at him as he lay on his back with his arms and legs extended thinking, this is almost a laugh. This "almost laugh" seemed to quickly turn into a hearty chuckle, which he still expressed into his toddlerhood. These laughs would be accompanied by direct eye contact which at around six months can be described as *purposeful joint attention*—Eli would often turn his eye gaze and attend to whatever object I was looking at.

As Table 2.1 shows, babbling alone goes through its own important process. Babbling begins to sound more speech-like around four to six months (at this age, Eli spent most of the time babbling the /b/ and /d/ sounds[1]). Around the age of seven months to one year, babbles begin to use long and short groups of sounds (for Eli, /d/ turned into a repeated "dada" pattern). At around this time, babbles might be a mix of two or more sounds like "ba be da." They are also more intentional; babies babble to get and keep someone's attention. Babbling usually continues after the first year, combined with real words and pseudo words. Eventually, babbling fades away and real words completely take over (although a dose of babbling might arise if a toddler or preschooler is engaged in pretend play and has taken on the role of a baby).

Infant speech development (speech perception and production) involves both receptive and expressive language skills. *Receptive language* has to do with a child's ability to understand what's being said, whereas *expressive language* refers to a child's use of verbal and non-verbal modes of communication to express their wants and needs. From an early age, children can typically understand more than what they can articulate; their receptive language skills develop faster than their expressive skills. At 16 months, Eli, for instance, would follow simple directions when asked to retrieve a particular book from the bookshelf or take his water bottle from the table for a suggested drink. Whether they're given verbally or through signs and gestures, understanding instructions is one way for a toddler to demonstrate their receptive language skills.

Other ways that parents and caregivers can promote receptive and expressive language development include *infant-directed speech* and *joint attention* activities. As I described earlier, infant-directed speech uses a high pitch, is slower, and often more melodic than usual. These exaggerated aspects of language get and keep a baby's attention and can let a baby know the emotional tone behind what's being communicated (Golinkoff et al., 2015). Joint attention activities might involve the infant and parent following the movement of an object like a spoon, toy car, or ball rolling across the floor. These types of shared and interactive activities support the development of language and social skills and can strengthen the bond between an infant and parent (Golinkoff et al., 2015). Following a parent or caregiver's gaze also has implications for understanding other people's points of views.

There are three developmental phases of joint attention: 1. Attendance to social partners, 2. Emergence and coordination of joint attention, and 3. Transition to language. Adamson and Chance (1998) provide key behaviours associated with each phase (see Figure 2.1).

In phase one (birth to six months), infants are receptive to interpersonal interactions, which can be both verbal and non-verbal. Infants at this phase are beginning to learn how to maintain attention for sustained periods of engagement. In phase two

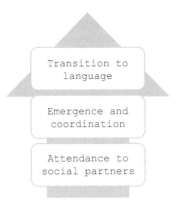

FIGURE 2.1 Phases of joint attention.

(6–12 months), joint attention between the caregiver and infant is more obvious and infants are more interested in noticing what their caregiver is looking at, particularly when the focus is on objects and images in the infant's environment, whether this is the shoe of a visiting family member or an illustration in a book. In phase three (one year and beyond), children typically have established joint attention and understand intentionality. Their social engagement with other individuals incorporates more mature communicative interactions.

It's both the quantity and the social-emotional aspect of these types of interactions or early "conversations" that are significant. As I noted in Chapter 1, infants are born ready to learn any language. When they come into the world, they take statistics of the language(s) that they hear most often, and before their first birthday, they become language-bound listeners (Kuhl, 2011). Over time, infants and babies start building sound maps; they begin to segment the speech they hear into individual phonemes or speech sounds and then into more meaningful words and phrases. They devote their attention to the prosodic and phonetic regularities of their language (Pence Turnbull & Justice, 2017); *prosodic* referring to the pitch, length, and loudness of sound and *phonetic* referring to those individual sounds in words, like the initial sound /c/ in the word *cat*. Nine-month-old infants surrounded by English speakers, for instance, prefer to listen to words containing a strong-weak stress pattern, like "**bark**ing **dogg**ie" and "**smil**ing **ba**by" (Pence Turnbull & Justice, 2017, p. 124). As infants hear their native language(s) more and more, they begin to develop the ability to recognize acceptable combinations of sounds in their language. Infants' ability to discriminate between speech sounds in their dominant language plays a significant role in later language development, affecting a child's ability to acquire words, morphology, and syntax (Kuhl et al., 2005).

But, as I indicated above, quantity is not the full story. It's not enough for an infant to only hear the repeated sounds and words of their native language. Researchers are clear that the socio-emotional aspect of language learning is also important (Kuhl, 2011). Patricia Kuhl demonstrated the significance of being present with your infant during "talk" in a study that looked at three different groups of six- and seven-month-old infants. Over 12 sessions three groups were given the same "dosage" of language; in the first group this language "dosage" was given directly by the caregiver, in the second group the infants received the same "dosage" over a television set, while the third-group of babies were exposed to the dosage of language through an audio recording while looking at a teddy bear on a screen. As you may have guessed, no learning occurred with the second and third group. Kuhl et al. concluded that human interaction is necessary for babies to learn language (2005).

The social relationship between the child and caregiver is essential to language development—making eye contact, following an infant's gaze, pointing and responding, repeating and imitating babbles, and describing objects that the infant is looking at all foster social interactions and ultimately, speech and language learning. In a review of studies that examined caregiver talk, social interactions and shared reading experiences were found to be most impactful when they were rich and varied and occurred in the context of an engaged and trusting adult–child social relationship (Zauche et al., 2016).

Oral language development continues beyond the toddler years, well into a child's school years. Engaging in conversations with parents, caregivers, and teachers expands a child's vocabulary, promotes active listening comprehension skills, and fosters appropriate conversational behaviours. As Table 2.1 shows, infants and toddlers achieve incredible feats before their second birthday. Some researchers even suggest that the time between birth and age three is the most intensive period for acquiring speech and language skills (NIDCD, 2022). It's during this time that the developing brain is best able to absorb language. Given a social environment rich in language, the awaiting brain begins learning language. While there may be variations in children's development of speech and language skills, there is indeed a natural progression for learning these skills (NIDCD, 2022). If you notice any significant discrepancies between the typical progression of speech and language development and your child's language behaviours, then it's important to speak to your family physician or paediatrician (NIDCD, 2022).

Shared reading

Shared reading is a highly effective way for parents and teachers to incorporate books into a social and interactive activity that promotes oral language development. Shared reading occurs between a caregiver and child and can start right from birth; the caregiver reads a book aloud and offers comments and questions about the story, author, or text structure, and the child responds. The main goals of shared reading are for the caregiver and child to engage in a conversation about the book through mainly open-ended questions (those that begin with "why" or "how", for instance), and for the child to begin to develop an understanding of print and build their skills in listening comprehension. During shared reading, if a parent or teacher points out print, a child will more likely attend to the words as they're read aloud; the child can begin to understand that the text plays a role in the story. The illustrations also play a significant role in shared reading, especially in the early years. As a child becomes more and more familiar with the text structures of different genres, they begin to understand the importance of print, that print conveys a message. Parents and caregivers can foster this early understanding by pointing out print, emphasizing or stressing words in the text, and asking young children to identify any familiar letter names or sounds they see in the text.

Of course, a child will increasingly respond and interact, and even ask their own questions, as their language skills develop; a parent or caregiver might only initially receive what seem like random coos and babbles from their two-month-old infant while they read aloud a board book. Starting to read to an infant early, however, sets up an important habit that research has shown to be tied to later reading comprehension (Ece Demir-Lira et al., 2019). Reading with your child should happen at different times during the day (don't just limit shared reading to your nighttime routine!). It's also another excellent way to foster the socio-emotional part of language learning. Cuddling up to read has been found to change the structure of a child's brain and the ways in which their brains make connections (Hutton et al., 2019). This seems to be especially true when parents engage in shared reading with illustrated books, as opposed to picture-less books or audio books. In a study by John Hutton et al. (2019), findings showed that books with supporting illustrations activated the language, visual, and attention networks of the brain. Research has also found that children who are read to often have larger vocabularies (Sénéchal et al., 2008), especially as text selection becomes more complex and new vocabulary is introduced (and talked about!). The benefits of shared reading also tap into reading fluency and comprehension skills. The caregiver is basically modelling fluent reading, reading aloud with expression and suitable prosody, and at an appropriate rate (more on this later in Chapter 7).

As infants become toddlers the interactions during shared reading can become more of a two-way street. And the questions a parent, caregiver, or teacher might ask can indeed vary. A good mnemonic to consider for which types of questions or prompts to use is the acronym CROWD (Whitehurst et al., 1988).

C: Completion prompts
R: Recall prompts
O: Open-ended prompts
W: Wh- questions
D: Distancing prompts

Completion prompts are incomplete sentences where part of the sentence is left out for the child to call out. The easiest way to do a completion prompt is to omit the last word of a sentence and let the child or group of children call out the word. Rhyming books or books with which the children are familiar are great for trying out a completion prompt. *Recall prompts* are those that ask the children questions about what has happened in the book. The children learn about story structure and sequencing with recall prompts, which you can incorporate in the middle or at the end of a book read aloud. *Open-ended prompts* include questions that usually begin with "why" or "why do you think." These types of prompts can allow a child to make connections between the text and their own experiences. Open-ended prompts can also allow children to make predictions or inferences based on what they already know about the story. *Wh- questions* include who, what, where, and when. These types of questions allow children to tell you what is happening in the text and can also be a great way to introduce new vocabulary. Finally, *distancing prompts* are those that ask children to relate worldly ideas to the text and provide children with opportunities to make connections between the book and real-world events and experiences.

When considering the CROWD acronym, we can think of shared reading as "dialogic reading" which emphasizes the dialogue aspect of the activity (Whitehurst et al., 1988). Thinking of it in this light puts the dialogue between the children and parent or teacher at the centre, where the book acts as a conversation starter. Take the book, *Voices in the Park* by Anthony Browne (1998). Even before opening the book a parent and their six-year-old child, let's say, can engage in a dialogue about the title and cover illustration, setting the stage for the story's narrative. As simple as asking, "What do you wonder when you hear the title of the book or look at the illustration?" or saying, "This book takes place in a park," followed by the question "What is your favourite thing to do at the park?" When you ask these types of questions before even opening a book, you're eliciting or activating prior knowledge, what the children already know about the topic; the connections they make between the text and their own experiences and background knowledge. Activating prior knowledge and helping children build this type of knowledge has been directly linked to reading comprehension (Kendeou et al., 2016). This certainly makes sense; the more you know about a topic, the more you'll understand the text you are reading.

For children still in their toddler years, a parent might pick up a more straightforward and repetitive book, like *The Very Hungry Caterpillar* by Eric Carle (1969). Questions might be more direct, asking the child to recall or even point out parts of the narrative, like, "What did the caterpillar eat on Monday?" After becoming familiar with the story pattern, a completion prompt might be something like, "But he was still ———," with the child enthusiastically completing the sentence with "hungry!" Knowing the CROWD mnemonic can certainly help vary the questions you ask during a read aloud. It's important to go through the book ahead of time and select about three to five places to stop in the book to ask one of the CROWD-type questions. It's also okay to read a book through without stopping at all, especially if the book is new to the children. Interacting with the group and stopping to pose questions during a read aloud can happen on repeated readings (yes, children love hearing some books read to them repeatedly!).

From the field: Promoting oral language

Shared reading was a topic of conversation during the discussions I had with teachers across programmatic and geographic contexts. All the teachers I talked to, regardless of where they taught and their school's philosophy, read books with their students. During these read alouds, the teacher would often stop at various places to ask a question or respond to an eager hand waving in the air. Questions sometimes were spur of the moment, but the teachers did speak about their purposeful planning, even when it came to the type of questions they would ask.

Language development and language-rich environments were at the core of each teacher's practice. This was certainly apparent when, during several school visits, I looked around and saw labels telling children the names of objects, postings of the children's names and other creations, book nooks, and writing centres with provocations for writing and mark-making. Like dialogic reading, activities were carefully planned and intentionally carried out—this type of intention can have a significant impact on a child's oral language development. Teachers I spoke to talked about how they purposefully selected books and materials that promoted rich language and used a variety of types of words. These teaching opportunities were direct and explicit, in both the planning and implementation. Intent is indeed important for supporting children's language development. Of course, language learning also occurs implicitly through children's ongoing interactions with print and spoken language.

Other ways in which parents and teachers can support a child, at any age, in their language development are included at the end of the chapter. Increasing "wait" or "think time" can be especially beneficial. Although it can be a challenge to sit in silence for even three seconds after asking a question, "wait time" has been shown to increase the chances of a child responding on a deeper level (Duncan & Lederberg, 2018; Rowe, 1986). We can be so quick to give a child (or another adult, for that matter) an answer or suggestion after posing a question; however, waiting for even a very brief period of time can give a child the confidence necessary to reply. This "wait time" also gives the child an opportunity to process the information and think about how they will articulate their response.

Emphasizing vocabulary is also key in supporting a child's language development and has been shown to directly impact reading comprehension (Baumann, 2009; Duke & Carlisle, 2011; Wagner, Muse, & Tannenbaum, 2007). Through shared reading, interactive conversations, and attending to new words and their meanings, parents and teachers can foster a child's knowledge of and interest in words. Their "word consciousness" develops, which directly connects back to growth in their oral language skills. I'll discuss word consciousness in Chapter 3, when I delve into vocabulary development. For now, the key take-away of Chapter 2 is that oral language development sets the foundation for continued language growth and early literacy skills. Providing children with a language-rich environment, right from birth, can have a positive effect on their oral language development.

Tips for supporting oral language development

0–24 months

- ◆ Respond to coos and babbles.
- ◆ Interact face-to-face.
- ◆ Follow gazes and make eye contact when speaking.
- ◆ Point out print in the environment.
- ◆ Identify signs and logos.
- ◆ Describe objects and events.
- ◆ Use simple directions.
- ◆ Sing songs and chant rhymes.
- ◆ Use and follow gestures.
- ◆ Follow the child's lead.
- ◆ Set aside time for shared reading every day.

2–8 years (and beyond)

- ◆ Extend a child's thinking by posing a question.
- ◆ Ask open-ended questions.
- ◆ Increase "wait" or "think time."
- ◆ Emphasize new vocabulary.
- ◆ Activate prior knowledge by making connections between the book and a child's experiences and knowledge.
- ◆ Set aside time for shared reading every day.
- ◆ Provide choice in book selection.
- ◆ Read books with a range of vocabulary.
- ◆ Follow a child's interest in book selection.
- ◆ Read fiction and non-fiction books.

Recommended books for fostering oral language development

- ◆ *A Flock of Shoes* by Sarah Tsiang
- ◆ *Amazing Grace* by Mary Hoffman
- ◆ *Butterfly Park* by Ely MacKay
- ◆ *Chicka Chicka Boom Boom* by Bill Martin Jr. & John Archambault

- *Chrysanthemum* by Kevin Hanke
- *Goodnight Moon* by Margaret Wise Brown
- *Moo, Baa, La La La* by Sandra Boynton
- *Owl Moon* by Jane Yolen
- *The Most Magnificent Thing* by Ashley Spires
- *The Very Hungry Caterpillar* by Eric Carle
- *Where's Spot* by Eric Hill
- *You Are Stardust* by Eline Kelsey

Note

1 Note that the backslashes indicate the sound of the letter rather than the letter name.

References

Adamson, L.B., & Chance, S.E. (1998). Coordinating attention to people, objects, and language. In: A.M. Wetherby, S.F. Warren, & J. Reichle (Eds.), *Transitions in prelinguistic communication: Preintentional to intentional and presymbolic to symbolic* (pp. 15–37). Baltimore: Brookes.

American Speech–Language–Hearing Association (ASHA). (2024). *Communication milestones*. https://www.asha.org/public/developmental-milestones/communication-milestones/

Baumann, J.F. (2009). Intensity in vocabulary instruction and effects on reading comprehension. *Topics in Language Disorders*, *29*(4), 312–328. https://doi.org/10.1097/TLD.0b013e3181c29e22

Brown, A. (1998). *Voices in the park*. Random House.

Carle, E. (1969). *The very hungry caterpillar*. World Publishing Company.

Duke, N.K., & Carlisle, J. (2011). The development of comprehension. In: *Handbook of reading research*, Volume IV (pp. 199–228). Routledge.

Demir-Lira, Ö., Applebaum, L.R., Goldin-Meadow, S., & Levine, S.C. (2019). Parents' early book reading to children: Relation to children's later language and literacy outcomes controlling for other parent language input. *Developmental Science*, *22*(3). https://doi.org/10.1111/desc.12764

Duncan, M.K., & Lederberg, A.R. (2018). Relations between teacher talk characteristics and child language in spoken-language deaf and hard-of-hearing classrooms. *Journal of Speech, Language, and Hearing Research, 61*(12), 2977–2995. https://doi.org/10.1044/2018_JSLHR-L-17-0475

Hutton, J.S., Dudley, J., Horowitz-Kraus, T., DeWitt, T., & Holland, S.K. (2019). Functional connectivity of attention, visual, and language networks during audio, illustrated, and animated stories in preschool-age children. *Brain Connectivity, 9*(7), 580–592. https://doi.org/10.1089/brain.2019.0679

Golinkoff, R.M., Can, D.D., Soderstrom, M., & Hirsh-Pasek, K. (2015). (Baby) talk to me: The social context of infant-directed speech and its effects on early language acquisition. *Current Directions in Psychological Science, 24*(5), 339–344. https://doi.org/10.1177/0963721415595345

Kendeou, P., McMaster, K.L., & Christ, T.J. (2016). Reading comprehension: Core components and processes. *Policy Insights from the Behavioral and Brain Sciences, 3*(1), 62–69. https://doi.org/10.1177/2372732215624707

Kuhl, P.K. (2011). Social mechanisms in early language acquisition: Understanding integrated brain systems supporting language. In: J. Decety & J.T. Cacioppo (Eds.), *The Oxford handbook of social neuroscience* (pp. 649–667). Oxford University Press.

Kuhl, P. K., Conboy, B.T., Padden, D., Nelson, T., & Pruitt, J. (2005). Early speech perception and later language development: Implications for the "critical period". *Language Learning and Development, 1*(3–4), 237–264. https://doi.org/10.1080/15475441.2005.9671948

Kuhl, P.K., & Meltzoff, A.N. (1996). Infant vocalizations in response to speech: Vocal imitation and developmental change. *The Journal of the Acoustical Society of America, 100*(4), 2425–2438.

National Institute on Deafness and Other Communication Disorders. (2022). *Speech and language developmental milestones.* https://www.nidcd.nih.gov/health/speech-and-language

Pence Turnbull, K., & Justice, L. (2017). *Language development from theory to practice (3rd edition).* Pearson.

Rowe, M.B. (1986). Wait time: Slowing down may be a way of speeding up! *Journal of Teacher Education, 37*(1), 43–50.

Sénéchal, M., Pagan, S., Lever, R., & Ouellette, G.P. (2008). Relations among the frequency of shared reading and 4-year-old children's vocabulary, morphological and syntax comprehension, and narrative skills. *Early Education and Development*, *19*(1), 27–44. https://doi.org/10.1080/10409280701838710

Wagner, R.K., Muse, A.E., & Tannenbaum, K.R. (2007). *Vocabulary acquisition: Implications for reading comprehension*. Guilford Press.

Whitehurst, G. J., Falco, F. L., Lonigan, C. J., Fischel, J. E., DeBaryshe, B. D., Valdez-Menchaca, M. C., & Caulfield, M. (1988). Accelerating language development through picture book reading. *Developmental Psychology*, *24*(4), 552.

Zauche, L.H., Thul, T.A., Mahoney, A.E.D., & Stapel-Wax, J.L. (2016). Influence of language nutrition on children's language and cognitive development: An integrated review. *Early Childhood Research Quarterly*, *36*, 318–333. https://doi.org/10.1016/j.ecresq.2016.01.015

3

Becoming Word Conscious

Vocabulary Development

It had been about a week or so following Eli's first birthday that
I really started to recognize a few words that he had been utter-
ing and appearing to associate with their actual meaning. Take
dog for instance: During a sunny fall morning at the breakfast
table, a gentle golden retriever named Gracie approached Eli as
he sat in his highchair (she was more likely looking for crumbs
than looking for a toddler's attention). As Gracie approached, Eli
made the initial sound /d/ followed by, what sounded like the
word *dog*, though perhaps more like *dug*. Eli repeated the word,
sound combination, babble (however you want to describe it) a
few times before Gracie turned and walked away. The adults in
the room all nodded in agreement that Eli had indeed said *dog*.
Other distinguishable words that appeared to be in Eli's *expressive vocabulary* at around his first birthday were *go, ball*, and *dada*.
Dada had been a top word for a while and seemed connected
to my partner, Matt, although Eli did babble this word when
any other person walked by. Like most babies or toddlers, Eli's
receptive language abilities (his ability to understand words) had
been building for some time. *Garbage* was a newer word that Eli
seemed to understand—I had been repeating *garbage* about 10
times as we took walks across the room to the trash bin or com-
post to throw something away.

DOI: 10.4324/9781032688558-3

Early vocabulary acquisition

Early vocabulary acquisition begins at home with parents and caregivers. In Chapter 2, I described how an infant's early speech and language skills including their gestures, coos, and babbles all set the course for speaking and understanding words and language, and eventually conversing in discernable words and sentences. As I mentioned in Chapter 2 when discussing oral language development, beginning to understand words, *receptive language*, happens before babies begin speaking, or before *expressive language* develops. Like Eli taking orders to throw away the garbage, babies begin following directions and understanding simple questions before or around their first birthday. In the 12-to-17-month range, babies typically begin initiating interactions and answering these simple questions, perhaps also responding "no" (or "yes" if your toddler is more agreeable) to the directions you've given them.

The words that babies, toddlers, and young children begin to understand grows at, what seems like, an exponential pace; by the time a child is nearing the end of second grade, for instance, they might understand over 6,000 root word meanings (a *root word* is any word that can stand alone and usually cannot be further divided into meaningful units—more about root words, suffixes and all things related to morphology in Chapter 4; Biemiller & Slonim, 2001). For each word, there is a mental representation about that word stored in the child's lexicon. This storage happens when a child really starts to know a word's meaning, how to use the word in a particular context, and how the word connects to other words. The child's *vocabulary depth* is expanding, where the child begins to understand multiple aspects of a word. Take the word *tiger*, for example: A child who knows the word *tiger* knows that this animal does more than just roar (although that's a good starting point). The child can identify that the word is part of a larger category (a tiger is an animal and related to other cat-like animals); they might connect the word *tiger* to other animals they've seen at the zoo or on a television show; and eventually, they might be able to talk about a *tiger* within the context of pre-serving the rainforest, for instance. Eventually, children develop even deeper understandings of a word. This happens when they begin to know the *orthography* of the word as well, how the word is spelled. Combined with phonology (how a word sounds) and semantics (what a word means), these three aspects—orthography, phonology, and semantics—form a "reading network" in the brain (Hadley & Dickinson, 2020; Kirby, 2019; Seidenberg & McClelland, 1989). When one aspect of the network is activated, this activation spreads strengthening the connections for individual words (Kirby, 2019).

Vocabulary depth is highly correlated with *vocabulary breadth*, which refers to all the words someone knows; it's the size of an individual's vocabulary, also known as a *lexicon* (think of the term *lexicon* as a mental representation of a dictionary). Research has shown that vocabulary breadth is more important for predicting decoding skills, whereas depth of vocabulary is more important for predicting reading comprehension skills (Ouellette, 2006). Both, however, contribute highly to a child's *word consciousness*, their knowledge of and interest in words (Schwanenflugel & Knapp, 2015). Word consciousness is thought to promote an understanding of how words and ideas are related and can be an especially important construct for fostering an enjoyment in learning new words.

Vocabulary development and the process of acquiring new words happen through both implicit and explicit learning opportunities. Implicit vocabulary learning occurs through everyday conversations and interactions with parents, caregivers, and other children. In fact, the number of words a child is exposed to has a direct effect on the size of their vocabulary and can play a significant role in later language learning and reading development (Rowe, 2012). A longitudinal study that looked at important predicators in vocabulary growth found that toddlers' vocabulary growth was influenced by the quantity of words they had been exposed to over the previous year (Rowe, 2012). The type of words also influenced toddlers' vocabularies; toddlers exposed to a variety of more higher-level and complex words[1] during the previous year showed greater gains in vocabulary development. Just as we've seen with oral language development, quantity is not the full story; exposing children to a variety of types of words and synonyms of familiar words, especially for children ages two to three, can play a significant role in vocabulary growth.

For the most part, toddlers' vocabulary development happens indirectly, through listening to new words they hear during conversations with adults. Similar to how parents can foster their child's speech development, parents and caregivers can also help their children expand their vocabulary through more explicit approaches (Biemiller, 2003). Emphasizing new words, repeating a word several times, using the word in different sentences, and even having the toddler repeat (or at least attempt to repeat) a new word are more explicit ways in which a parent can foster vocabulary development. By the time your toddler is two, they might even start asking you to identify and label objects in their environment or images in a book they're reading. Their natural curiosity and interest in the world around them could indeed be a catalyst for regular bouts of "what's that?" (we'll turn our attention to morphology and syntax development in Chapter 4, where the discussion of more complex utterances and phrases will continue).

From the field: Vocabulary learning in a Montessori classroom

Vocabulary learning and supporting word consciousness were topics of conversation in my discussions with teachers from across early years programmes. A Montessori teacher I met in Mexico City, for instance, spent a lot of time speaking about the importance of introducing and talking about words with the young children she taught. She, like all the teachers I spoke with over the course of the year, was passionate about language and early literacy development, and it was clear that vocabulary was a critical component of her literacy programme. Vocabulary was a particularly prominent aspect of this teacher's literacy programme because this teacher was an English teacher to mostly Spanish-speaking kindergarten children. I was fortunate to observe this teacher work with a small group of children on a vocabulary-building activity, in which she introduced the English names of familiar objects to her kindergarten students. Each object was explicitly named and described in relation to other objects laid out on the table. She also asked the children if they had an experience with the object she was holding, providing them with an opportunity to connect the new word to already familiar words and ideas. All these strategies have been shown to be highly effective. Explicitly naming objects, connecting new words to familiar words, and describing and providing examples of the object allows children to develop vocabulary depth.

Marzano (2004) suggests six steps to follow when teaching new vocabulary:

1. Pre-select a word from an upcoming text or conversation.
2. Explain the meaning with student-friendly definitions.
3. Provide examples of how it is used.
4. Ask students to repeat the word three times.
5. Engage students in activities to develop proficiency.
6. Ask students to say the word again.

Provide explicit vocabulary instruction

Whether it's in their first, second, or fifth language, supporting children's vocabulary development by explicitly discussing the meaning of words, talking about words in relation to other similar words, and sharing ways to use words in sentences and broader contexts are all essential aspects for understanding texts and media. The teachers I talked to over the course of the year certainly knew the value of what it takes to really know a word and foster word consciousness; they continuously encouraged conversations, read to their students, and had their students read often. Books and other forms of media can introduce children to new words that we don't necessarily use in our day-to-day conversations. Take the author Roald Dahl, for instance. In his classic chapter books, like *James and Giant Peach* (Dahl, 1961) and *Charlie and the Chocolate Factory* (Dahl, 1964), Dahl uses fantastical adjectives for the reader to create vivid images and understand the text in greater complexity. I love the words Dahl (1961) uses in this paragraph from *James and the Giant Peach*:

> They all watched, aghast. And now at a signal from the leader all the other sharks came swimming in toward the peach and they clustered around it and began to attack it furiously. There must have been twenty or thirty of them at least, all pushing and fighting and lashing their tails and churning the water into a froth.
>
> (p. 56)

Words like *aghast, clustered, furiously, lashing, churning*, and *froth* could easily be replaced by more common words (*aghast* could have been *scared, churning* could have been *mixing*), but Dahl ensures his readers are engaged in the story by opting for the use of higher-level vocabulary.

Beck et al. (2013) have suggested three tiers of vocabulary words (see Figure 3.1). The words listed above (aghast, clustered, furiously, etc.) can be described as tier two words and can be taught explicitly. Instruction in these words can add productively to an individual's language ability. Beck et al. (2013) suggest that teachers select tier two words based on the following criteria:

- ◆ *Importance and utility*: words that are characteristic of mature language users and appear across a variety of domains.
- ◆ *Instructional potential*: words that can be worked within a variety of ways so that students can build rich representations of them and their connections to other words and concepts.
- ◆ *Conceptual understanding*: words for which students understand the general concept but provide precision and specificity in describing the concept.

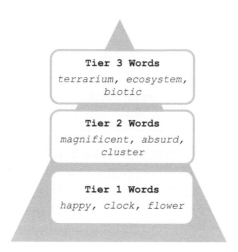

FIGURE 3.1 Three tires of vocabulary words.

Kucan (2012) also provides guidelines for identifying tier two words:

♦ Look for words that can be used across domains.
♦ Ask yourself whether your students have knowledge or experiences that would help them understand the word.
♦ Consider whether the word is useful and important to comprehension.

Tier one words, as you may have guessed, are words that are more common and can be dealt with quickly, like *happy*, *clock*, and *flower*. These words are likely concrete words and don't necessarily need to be taught explicitly with English-speaking students since they likely already know these familiar words. Children learning English as an additional language typically know tier one words in their native language, so they understand the concept of the words; they should be provided with direct instruction on tier one words and should quickly pick up on the meaning and use of these words (Biemiller & Slonim, 2001). Tier three words are words that are usually used in specific domains. *Terrarium*, *ecosystem*, and *biosphere*, for example, are words that might come up during a specific science lesson. Of course, there are too many words that fall under each category to teach directly. However, explicit instruction within an appropriate context can indeed support children's vocabulary development (Biemiller, 2003).

Knowledge of tier two words can have a huge impact on someone's oral and written language, so selecting these types of words to teach directly is extremely useful. During a read aloud, for instance, a teacher might introduce the word *enormous* to their kindergarten students. The teacher might touch the word and say, "this word says *enormous*," then have their students say it altogether. The teacher might then tell the students what it means: "Enormous means very large." With their students, the teacher might then ask if there are other words that mean very large. They might also use the word in a sentence or play *I Spy* and find objects around the classroom that are enormous. The students would likely already have a concept of enormous, the teacher's role is to help the students make the connection between a word the students are already familiar with (*big* perhaps) and the new higher-level word. While you might introduce a new word through this approach a few times a week, be sure to repeat the word in different contexts and have the children practise using the word throughout the day. For children who might struggle remembering the word's meaning, visual images or cues can help. And for those children who already know the word you're introducing, have them consider another synonym (or more!) for the word you've introduced. Concept maps are a great visual representation to see the connections between synonyms (see Figure 3.2).

Other ideas for teaching the meaning of a word explicitly include:

◆ Visualizing the word,
◆ Creating an illustration of the word,
◆ Previewing vocabulary before reading, and
◆ Using the arts as an avenue for further exploration of a word.

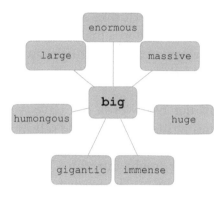

FIGURE 3.2 Concept map for the word *big*.

This last idea could involve "word painting," which is a technique that composers sometimes use to metaphorically paint a word with sound and musical gesture (Beach & Bolden, 2019). When a new word is introduced, students are invited to paint or illustrate the word in a way that communicates how they imagine a performance of that word might sound. As with the other arts, music can act as a memory aid when learning the meaning of new words. Music helps us remember things because we perceive it both cognitively and affectively; musical experiences impact us on an affective level; music makes us feel (Levitin, 2006). Painting a word involves the visual representation of how the word might sound; students connect a newly learned word to a visual and sonic representation that they create themselves and is directly connected to the word's meaning. For instance, students might paint the word *exciting* on an upward slant to indicate pitch getting higher (Figure 3.3).

New and interesting words that students come across, either through a book being read aloud, during a conversation with a peer or adult, or while watching a favourite show, can be compiled into a "word collector." When I taught grade three, a "word collector" was located beside our gathering place where we often met for group lessons and read alouds. The word collector was basically a sheet of chart paper posted on the wall with designated areas organized alphabetically. If a goal during a read aloud was to listen for new and interesting words, hands would

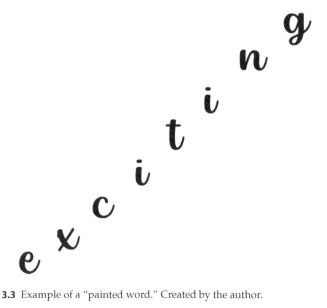

FIGURE 3.3 Example of a "painted word." Created by the author.

eagerly wave as I read from a chapter book and my students would be ready to list off words they heard me read. Any new word would go onto the word collector and then a discussion about the word would ensue. The words on the word collector would sometimes find their way into the students' writing, especially when the students would jot down the new words in their own personal word collector they housed in their file folders.

All these strategies help children know a word, even very young children who can't yet read the word. Fostering word consciousness for children in the pre-alphabetic phase of word learning development, where they have not yet grasped sound–symbol relationships (Ehri, 1999), still has direct implications for language development. Vocabulary development and understanding the meaning of words relate to the side of *the simple view of reading* dedicated to language comprehension and directly link to background knowledge and, ultimately, reading comprehension (Hoover & Gough, 1990). When a teacher provides student-friendly definitions, discusses examples and non-examples of words, teaches multiple meanings, and links new words to words students already know, their students are becoming word conscious. The hope is that by fostering word consciousness, students are not only acquiring knowledge of words but they're also gaining an interest in words. When children are curious about words and have an awareness of the impact word choice can have on how a message is conveyed, their vocabulary is more likely to expand leading to improved communication and, ultimately, reading comprehension.

Tips for supporting vocabulary development at any age

- ◆ Point out and talk about new words in books and other forms of media.
- ◆ Use objects and illustrations to introduce new words.
- ◆ Emphasize or stress new words.
- ◆ Repeat new words several times.
- ◆ Provide child-friendly definitions.
- ◆ Relate new words to familiar words.
- ◆ Connect new words to familiar ideas and experiences.
- ◆ Create concept maps and illustrations.
- ◆ Use word painting to musically represent the word.
- ◆ Incorporate a "word of the day" into your daily routine.

Recommended books for supporting vocabulary development

- ◆ *Click, Clack, Moo, Cows That Type* by Doreen Cronen
- ◆ *Don't Let the Pigeon Drive Us* by Mo Williams
- ◆ *Giraffes Can't Dance* by Giles Andreae
- ◆ *Interrupting Chicken* by Ezra Stein
- ◆ *James and the Giant Peach* by Roald Dahl
- ◆ *Lon Po Po* by Ed Young
- ◆ *Max's Castle* by Kate Banks
- ◆ *Nokum Is My Teacher* by David Bouchard
- ◆ *The Cardinal and the Crow* by Michael Moniz
- ◆ *The True Story of the Three Little Pigs* by Jon Scieszka
- ◆ *The Word Collector* by Peter H. Reynolds

Note

1 Higher-level complex words can be described as synonyms for familiar words and words that you don't necessarily use in everyday conversations.

References

Beach, P., & Bolden, B. (2019). Word painting: A creative way to enhance vocabulary. *The Reading Teacher, 72*(6), 750–754. https://doi.org/10.1002/trtr.1780

Beck, I.L., McKeown, M.G., & Kucan, L. (2013). *Bringing words to life: Robust vocabulary instruction*. Guilford Press.

Biemiller, A., & Slonim, N. (2001). Estimating root word vocabulary growth in normative and advantaged populations: Evidence for a common sequence of vocabulary acquisition. *Journal of Educational Psychology, 93*, 498–520.

Biemiller, A. (2003). Vocabulary: Needed if more children are to read well. *Reading Psychology, 24*(3–4), 323–335.

Dahl, R. (1964). *Charlie and the chocolate factory*. George Allen & Unwin.

Dahl, R. (1961). *James and the giant peach*. Alfred A. Knopf.

Ehri, L.C. (1999). Phases of development in learning to read words. In: J. Oakhill & R. Beard (Eds.), *Reading development and the teaching of reading: A psychological perspective* (pp. 79–108). Blackwell Science.

Hadley, E.B., & Dickinson, D.K. (2020). Measuring young children's word knowledge: A conceptual review. *Journal of Early Childhood Literacy, 20*(2), 223–225. https://doi.org/10.1177/1468798417753713

Hoover, W.A., & Gough, P.B. (1990). The simple view of reading. *Reading and Writing, 2*, 127–160.

Kirby, J.R. (2019). Word knowledge quality and literacy. In: J. Orrell & H. Askell-Williams (Eds.), *Problem solving for teaching and learning: A festschrift in honour of Emeritus Professor Mike Lawson* (pp. 48–66). New York: Routledge.

Kucan, L. (2012). What is most important to know about vocabulary? *The Reading Teacher, 65*(6), 360–366. https://doi.org/10.1002/TRTR.01054

Levitin, D.J. (2006). *This is your brain on music: The science of a human obsession*. Penguin.

Marzano, R.J. (2004). *Building background knowledge for academic achievement: Research on what works in schools*. Association for Supervision and Curriculum Development. https://files.ascd.org/staticfiles/ascd/pdf/siteASCD/video/buildingacademic.pdf

Ouellette, G.P. (2006). What's meaning got to do with it: The role of vocabulary in word reading and reading comprehension. *Journal of Educational Psychology*, *98*(3), 554–566. https://doi.org/10.1037/0022-0663.98.3.554

Rowe, M. (2012). A longitudinal investigation of the role of quantity and quality of child-directed speech in vocabulary development. *Child Development*, *83*(5), 1762–1774. https://doi.org/10.1111/j.1467-8624.2012.01805.x

Schwanenflugel, P.J., & Knapp, N.F. (2015). *The psychology of reading: Theory and applications*. Guilford Publications.

Seidenberg, M. S., & McClelland, J. L. (1989). A distributed, developmental model of word recognition and naming. *Psychological Review*, *96*(4), 523–568.

4

Fostering Word Scientists

Language Syntax and Morphology

A few days before Eli's second birthday, I came home from teaching a class around the start of our dinner time. I was welcomed at the door by a cheery almost-two-year-old and invited in with the greeting, "Come in mommy." I was then informed that "Daddy's making dinner" which was indeed apparent from the delicious aroma that filled the house. This was followed by the statement, "I ate strawberries" which was also quite apparent given the red stains on Eli's face and t-shirt. Each of these sentences was said with certainty and confidence and provided insight into the current and recent happenings at home. As we approached Eli's second birthday, almost adult-like conversations were occurring where there was an exchange of ideas, questions, and responses between myself or my partner, Matt, and Eli. While these conversations were sometimes negotiations about how much longer Eli could play at the park or whether socks needed to stay on or off, Eli's sentences that formed these conversations comprised of organized words and simple, but meaningful, phrases. Eli had been combining words for several months, starting around 16 to 18 months or so. It was around the 20-month mark that he began stringing three and four words together and "conversing" with any listening ear.

DOI: 10.4324/9781032688558-4

Early syntax development

Typically, syntax or the development of sentence structure begins around 24 months where words a toddler combines might include objects, actions, and descriptors or adjectives (Lowry, 2018). You might refer to toddlers at this stage of syntax development as *word combiners*. By around 30 months, toddlers begin using more complete and adult-like sentences (Lowry, 2018); we might call toddlers at this stage *early sentence formers*. The main difference between the ability to combine words and create more complete sentences is that early sentences require at least a subject and a verb (Lowry, 2016). A toddler using early sentences with subjects and verbs might still be missing some adult-like grammar, but they are certainly on their way to becoming a *complete sentence user* (see Figure 4.1 for a visual of these stages of syntax development). Take the following examples from Eli's early toddler days:

Go fast.
More macaroni.
Mommy stay.
I need water bottle.
Daddy is in the kitchen.
I want cookie.

Eli became a *word combiner* when he started saying things like "go fast" and "more macaroni." These first two examples from the list are missing a subject (a person, place, or thing), so while we understand the message and can easily respond, on a technical level, they aren't quite complete sentences. The other four examples from the list have at least a subject and a verb, telling us a bit more about Eli's complete thoughts. A toddler transitioning to a

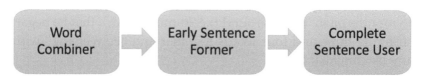

FIGURE 4.1 Syntax development.

full *early sentence former* still combines words, like in the first two examples, but as their ability to form full and complete sentences grows, they are indeed well on their way to more adult-like conversations and becoming proficient in the subject-verb-object order on which English grammar is based.

You may also hear toddlers at this stage in their syntax development use (and repeat) expressions they hear from the adults around them (Lowry, 2016). Eli would often say "thank you" and "you're welcome" in the same breath if, for instance, he was given a toy or a snack to eat. He had an understanding that these two expressions worked together, he just hadn't yet grasped their correct usage. Other expressions that he had memorized around his second birthday included "I did it," "there we go," and "I see it." Along with these memorized expressions, Eli didn't always use the correct subject. If he wanted me or my partner to pick him up, for instance, he would say "I carry you," even though he was indeed the one who wanted to be carried. These types of errors are part of the progression of syntax development, which is why it's important for parents and caregivers not to feel upset by mistakes or to be quick to correct a toddler's grammar (although you can certainly repeat the correct grammar—just avoid saying things like, "that's not right").

It's also important to use and refer to a variety of subjects in your sentences when conversing with a toddler. You can sometimes talk in the third person (for example, "Mommy is going to pick you up now"), particularly during the earlier stages of language development when a child is learning about who is who in the world and what we're all called. Using a variety of subjects during conversations (and speaking with a higher pitch and more exaggerated tone, similar to infant-directed speech that I described in Chapter 2) can boost a child's vocabulary and provide good examples of syntax and grammar, which is what they need for their implicit learning of sentence structure (Lowry, 2016). Here is a list of the pronouns toddlers typically learn at different ages (Keffer Hatleli, 2023):

- ◆ 1-year olds: Me, my, mine, you, it, that
- ◆ 2-year-olds: I, we, he, she, your, yours, this

- ◆ 3-year-olds: they, us, his, hers, them, her, him, our, myself, yourself, ours, their, theirs
- ◆ 4-year-olds: herself, himself, itself, ourselves, yourselves, themselves

As I've mentioned before, these typical milestones are just rough guidelines. You should speak to your family physician or a speech language pathologist if you have any concerns about your child's language development.

As children begin to speak using more adult-like sentence structure, they start to elaborate phrases by combining adjectives with nouns ("I see a fast car" where *car* is the noun and *fast* is the adjective) and adverbs with verbs ("She sings loudly" where *sings* is the verb and *loudly* is the adverb). This leads to the use of other more elaborate aspects of sentence structure including the use of coordinating conjunctions, like *and*, *or*, and *but* to combine phrases (or clauses), as well as the use of subordinating conjunctions, like *because*, *although*, and *despite*. With this last group of conjunctions, these words join independent and dependent clauses (phrases that depend on an independent phrase), whereas the first group of conjunctions usually join two or more independent clauses (phrases that can stand alone).

Before toddlers start combining words and forming sentences, they do need to be able to say quite a few words and say at least a few verbs, like *sit*, *come*, and *go* (Lowry, 2016). In fact, many children can say at least 40 verbs by the two-year mark (Lowry, 2016)—a huge developmental feat over a relatively short period of time. To help your child combine words speech-language pathologist, Lowry, suggests the following (2016):

1. Emphasize a variety of words including new words that are based on your child's interests. Highlight words by using actions and your voice so that new words stand out.
2. Model short grammatical sentences to help your child understand how words are used together and what the words mean.

3. Expand your child's words by repeating single words in a short sentence.
4. Follow your child's lead by letting your child lead the interaction. This can help your child feel motivated to communicate with you.

Prior to entering school, children typically acquire syntax implicitly, learning the broad grammatical rules of their language as they learn to understand what they hear and speak (Lowry, 2016). Each stage of syntax development gives children new opportunities to hone their communication skills and increase both their expressive and receptive oral language skills. I briefly discussed receptive and expressive language in Chapter 2. It's quite common for a child's *receptive language* (their ability to listen to and understand language) to develop before their *expressive language* (their ability to speak and express their ideas). Given this typical developmental order, it's important for parents and caregivers to continue using complete and complex sentences during conversations with babies and toddlers. There is no need to downplay grammar and sentences to match the two-word ungrammatical sentences a toddler might use. While you still want to be direct and keep your sentences as simple as possible, speaking with well-formed and grammatically correct sentences is, in part, how children learn the rules and structure of their language or dialect.

Morphology and morphological awareness

Syntax is one of the main language components that makes up grammar, the system and structure of language. Another component of language is morphology, the structure or form of words. With both syntax and morphology, we can consider the language side of *the simple view of reading*. Both are indeed aspects of oral language that, as I mentioned in previous chapters, begin to develop early in a child's life. Both syntax and morphology can also connect to decoding or print-related skills. As we'll see later in this chapter, when learning to read words and understanding texts, knowing about sentence structure and grammar, or syntax and morphology, can contribute to decoding skills and reading comprehension.

Morphemes are the smallest meaningful units of grammar within language. *Bases, prefixes,* and *suffixes* are types of morphemes in English. For instance, the word *playful* has two morphemes: *play* and *-ful. Play* is the base and can stand alone, so we can call it a *free base.* The suffix is *-ful* and means *full of.* A free base is a base that can stand on its own, like *play,* whereas a bound base is a base that cannot stand on its own, like *struct.* Bound bases must have a prefix, suffix, or another base added to it to make a word. If you add the suffix *-ure* to the bound base *struct* you get the word *structure.* Table 4.1 lists several common prefixes and suffixes with base word examples.

Morphological awareness is children's "conscious awareness of the morphemic structure of words and their ability to reflect on and manipulate that structure" (Carlisle, 1995, p. 194). To put it another way, when children develop morphological awareness, they can reflect on, analyse, and manipulate the morphemic elements in words. Morphological awareness typically begins when children start to develop an awareness and understanding that words containing more than one morpheme can be broken

TABLE 4.1 Common prefixes and suffixes with examples

Prefixes		Suffixes	
un-	unhappy, unsold, undone	-s	loves, grows, contains
pre-	preselect, precaution, preabsorb	-es	presses, bunches, beaches
dis-	disappear, discomfort, disagree	-ed	cared, melted, jumped
re-	redo, recreate, reread	-ing	telling, lasting, walking
in-	invoke, independent, involve	-ful	playful, careful, watchful
sub-	submarine, subject, subscribe	-ness	sharpness, dimness, tightness
super-	superficial, superimpose, supersonic	-ly	quietly, mostly, quickly
de-	decode, deconstruct, deactivate	-ist	artist, scientist, cartoonist
con-	conjecture, confess, consensus	-ure	composure, nurture, future
mist-	mistake, mistrust, misuse	-ism	altruism, opportunism, organism

down into smaller units and that *affixes* (prefixes and suffixes) can be added to bases to make new words with new meanings; likely beginning with inflections, as in the suffix *-s* (Kirby et al., 2012). For instance, take the word *replaying*. We can divide *replaying* into three morphemes—the base is *play* and can stand on its own, while *re* and *-ing* are affixes (*re* is a prefix and *-ing* is a suffix) and need to be attached to a base word to function and provide meaning.

There are also terms that describe how the meaning of a word has changed as a result of combining bases, prefixes, and suffixes. These are *inflections, derivations*, and *compounds. Inflections* are word endings that change the grammatical role, like adding *-s* for plurals and *-ed* for past tenses (e.g., the plural of *cat* is *cats*, the past tense of *walk* is *walked*). *Derivations* are words that combine bases with a prefix or non-inflectional suffix, like *pleasant* which is composed of the base word *please* and the suffix *-ant*; and *compound words* are words that include two or more bases, like the word *sunshine*—in this example each base or morpheme (*sun* and *shine*) can stand on its own. At around the age of two, it was quite interesting to hear Eli work through these different types of morphemes, even though he hadn't yet developed an explicit awareness of how we can break down words into their meaningful units. In fact, most adults are likely to be quite skilled in the realm of morphology without being conscious of it (J. R. Kirby, personal communication, January 31, 2024). Eli would repeat a plural noun several times in a row as though he was trying to grasp pluralities. Or after hearing or saying a word with the plural ending *-es* as in the word *buses*, Eli would then misuse and mispronounce the suffix *-es* in a word that only required *-s*, like *truckes*.

Supporting growth in syntax and morphology

As I mentioned earlier in the chapter, syntax and morphology are both language-related and print-related skills and can be particularly useful when a child is learning to decode (read) or encode (write) a word. Research on syntactic and morphological development and instruction has advanced over the past several decades, and there is a growing consensus that there is no need to wait until third or fourth grade to teach these skills (Kirby & Bowers, 2017). This might have been the approach in the past, that children in kindergarten and primary grades are not "ready" to learn more complex aspects of language and literacy. However, studies show that teaching syntax and morphology to children in kindergarten and the primary grades can have a positive impact on their reading skills in later grades (Kirby & Bowers, 2017). So, what does effective instruction in syntax and morphology look like at home and in the classroom? Let's start with syntax.

Teaching syntax from an early age means that children build on their implicit understanding of syntax and continue to learn about the structure of English and the rules that govern the ways in which words and phrases are arranged. Parents and teachers can improve a child's implicit understanding of the way in which grammar works, and knowing about how sentences work can indeed help readers with increasingly complex texts; messages in sentences are better understood when students understand sentence structure. There are many studies that show a direct relationship between understanding syntax and reading comprehension (e.g., Cain, 2007; Deacon & Kieffer, 2018; Goodwin, Petscher, & Reynolds, 2022; Mackay et al., 2021). For instance, Mackay et al. (2021) explored the role of syntax in reading comprehension of 11-year-olds. They found that understanding even just basic sentences made an important contribution to their reading comprehension. A few ideas for teaching syntax at home as well as across the primary grades include having children identify the parts of a sentence, build sentences (and break them down), and combine and expand sentences to extend ideas and sentence details.

Identifying parts of a sentence

Activities to support children in identifying parts of sentences or speech are not new and can indeed be helpful in supporting children's development and understanding of syntax. When planning such an activity consider the children's interests and allow for choice as much as possible. This could mean that the sentences you and your child or students work and play with include a bit of humour or are based on a topic of interest. Take this sentence: *My smooth green turtle crept under her chair while we played a game*. After introducing this sentence (reading it aloud and showing the written form) ask a series of simple questions about the sentence: Who did it? What did it do? What kind or how many there were? Where did it go? When did the event happen? Through this back-and-forth dialogue, children can start identifying the parts of the sentence (the noun, verb, adjectives, adverbs). You might consider adding picture cards with each key question word, which can be helpful for young children in the pre-alphabetic phase and children learning English as an additional language. Also, begin with just two options (e.g., the "who"—noun—and the "do"—verb) rather than all parts of the sentence. Picture cards and fewer options can help reduce a child's cognitive load,[1] saving energy to focus on and figure out the parts of the sentence (Torcasio & Sweller, 2010).

Building sentences

Building sentences can also make use of key question word cards or picture cards. Scaffold or support your children's learning by mixing up the word cards and having them put the cards into the correct order. For example:

> *ran quickly brown dog the*
> *The brown dog ran quickly.*

Select sentences from familiar books or passages and slowly add more words or images that represent the word to the scrambled sentences for increasing complexity. To increase children's motivation, have them select or create sentences themselves, or have them write down words on cards or draw pictures to scramble and rewrite into new (and interesting) sentences.

Combining and expanding sentences

I always enjoyed expanding sentences with my grade three students, especially when they were given the choice of words and ideas we would use for extensions—this usually led to giggles and a bit of silliness, but also learning and the children were indeed engaged. When expanding sentences, you might begin with the simple sentence: *The dog ran.* From there you can have children fill in details and elaborate on the ideas based on those same key question words I listed earlier. Here is an example of a detailed sentence of the dog that could have resulted from a brainstorm session with a group of third grade students: *The furry brown dog ran quickly across the field during a soccer game.*

Morphology instruction

Approaches to teaching morphology, particularly at the elementary level, include word sums and word matrices, and structured word inquiry also known as scientific word investigation. With any of these strategic approaches, it's important to keep in mind that as the parent or teacher you're trying to allow your children and students to build their word consciousness and see themselves as *word scientists*; help them develop their skills in morphology while at the same time develop an interest in words and word meanings. Becoming a *word scientist* means that children are using their morphological skills and awareness to understand and make sense of the English spelling and grammar systems.

Word sums and word matrices

Word sums and word matrices are effective and engaging ways for children to practise identifying morphemes in words. Word sums are like mathematical equations where you can break apart (and add up) morphemes in a given word. Using word equations or word sums is a great way to show the individual morphemes of a word. Here are four examples of word sums using the root word *struct* (meaning *to build*):

con + struct = construct
de + struct + ive = destructive
sub + struct + ure = substructure
struct + ure + al + ism = structuralism

Note that in the last example, *structuralism*, the first suffix *-ure* shows an action or result, and since there is a suffix that follows it, *-al*, we drop the *e*.

Word matrices work in a similar way, where the goal is to break down morphemes in words. This time, however, we can brainstorm as many prefixes and suffixes as possible that can be joined together with a given base to make a new word. Using the same base as above, *struct*, Figure 4.2 shows an example of a word matrix.

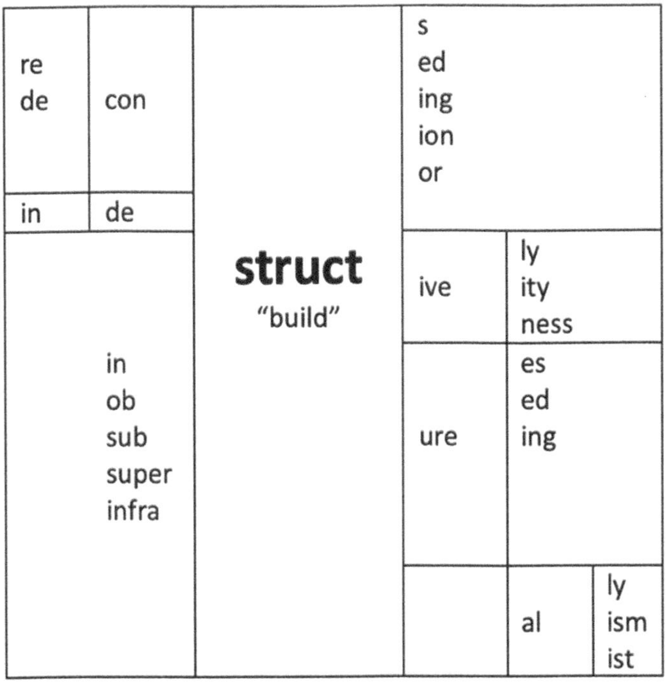

re de	con	**struct** "build"	s ed ing ion or	
in	de			
	in ob sub super infra		ive	ly ity ness
			ure	es ed ing
			al	ly ism ist

FIGURE 4.2 A word matrix example.

Rules for reading the words in any word matrix are to read from left to right, words must contain the base, and when you read across from left to right you cannot pass over a column. Word matrices can be used in simple (yet effective) games, such as timing students to make as many words as they can using a word matrix, word matrix bingo in which an affix is called out and students identify whether they have that affix on their bingo card, and word matrix puzzles in which students connect the affix and base-word cards to create new words.

Structured word inquiry

Structured word inquiry (SWI), also known as scientific word investigation, was first introduced by Pete Bowers and John Kirby in 2010 as an approach to teach morphology. In SWI four key questions can help set up an investigation of the spelling of a word:

1. What is the sense and meaning of your word?
2. How is it constructed? (Identify any bases or affixes with a word sum).
3. What related words can you find? (Morphological relatives, etymological[2] relatives)
4. How are the graphemes functioning in your word?

Using these questions to teach vocabulary, spelling, and word structure can be highly motivating for children across the grades increasing their word consciousness. In their 2010 study, Bower and Kirby asked grade four and five students to act as word detectives to investigate sets of words to reveal a targeted spelling pattern. Over the course of 20 lessons, the students worked through several spelling patterns where they formed and tested hypotheses about interesting ways in which some words are spelled (e.g., *sign*). A key component of the structured word inquiry process is investigating the history of the word, or the word's origins also known as *etymology*. Learning about the language(s) from which English words originated and how the word's meaning has evolved over time can be particularly engaging for children and elementary students. It can also help with understanding particular spelling patterns. A fantastic resource for finding out about word origins is Etymology Online (https://www.etymonline.com/). Pete Bowers also has an excellent list of resources for teaching about etymology and morphology on the website, Word Works Kingston (https://www.wordworkskingston.com/WordWorks/Home.html).

Incorporating inquiry, investigations, and children's interests into learning about words fosters word scientists. When children have opportunities to engage with words and sentences at a deeper level, they are more likely to develop an interest in learning about words and the rules that govern English grammar. This, in turn, will help increase vocabulary, solidify spelling skills, and develop reading comprehension. Helping children develop their syntax and morphology can also boost their confidence and conversational skills. By supporting children's implicit understanding of syntax and morphology at a young age, as well as providing them with explicit games and activities to increase their grammatical skills, we are helping them build their oral language skills, and over time, their reading skills too.

Tips for supporting syntax development

♦ Use and refer to a variety of subjects in your sentences during conversations.

♦ Restate sentences with correct grammar (but avoid correcting mistakes or saying "that's not right").

♦ When talking to your infant or toddler use a higher pitch and more exaggerated tone (infant-directed speech).

♦ Use a variety of words during conversations and add stress to new words for emphasis.

♦ Model short grammatical sentences to help your child understand how words are used together and what the words mean.

♦ Repeat words in a short sentence to expand vocabulary (and whenever possible, point out objects of these new words).

♦ Build sentences with word or picture cards.
♦ Use songs and familiar rhymes to increase interest and engagement.

Tips for supporting morphological development

♦ Use grammatically correct sentences with your child at any age.
♦ When a child uses the wrong inflectional ending or tense (e.g., truck**es** instead of trucks), repeat the correct word ending in a new sentence.
♦ Play rhyming games where you change or add a suffix to a familiar word.
♦ Add plural suffixes to objects through counting games.
♦ Create a list or concept map of words that all use the same prefix or suffix.
♦ Incorporate simple morphology lessons and activities into the classroom as early as preschool and kindergarten.

Recommended books for supporting syntax and morphology

♦ *A Is for Angry* by Sandra Boynton
♦ *A Lime, a Mime, a Pool Full of Slime* by Brian P. Cleary
♦ *Exclamation Mark* by Amy Krouse Rosenthal
♦ *Fantastic! Wow! and Unreal!: A Book About Interjections and Conjunctions* by Ruth Heller
♦ *If You Were a Noun* by Michael Dahl
♦ *Kites Sail High* by Ruth Heller
♦ *Nouns and Verbs Have a Field Day* by Robin Pulver
♦ *The Most Magnificent Thing* by Ashely Spires
♦ *Yo! Yes?* by Chris Raschka

Notes

1 Cognitive load refers to the amount of information our working memory can process during a given task.
2 Etymology is the study of the origin of words.

References

Bowers, P.N., & Kirby, J.R. (2010). Effects of morphological instruction on vocabulary acquisition. *Reading and Writing*, *23*, 515–537.

Cain, K. (2007). Syntactic awareness and reading ability: Is there any evidence for a special relationship? *Applied Psycholinguistics*, *28*(4), 679–694.

Carlisle, J.F. (1995). Morphological awareness and early reading achievement. In: L.B. Feldman (Ed.), *Morphological aspects of language processing* (pp. 189–209). Hillsdale, NJ: Erlbaum.

Deacon, S.H., & Kieffer, M. (2018). Understanding how syntactic awareness contributes to reading comprehension: Evidence from mediation and longitudinal models. *Journal of Educational Psychology*, *110*(1), 72–86.

Goodwin, A.P., Petscher, Y., & Reynolds, D. (2022). Unraveling adolescent language & reading comprehension: The monster's data. *Scientific Studies of Reading*, *26*(4), 305–326.

Keffer Hatleli, S. (2023, November 5). Understanding toddler pronoun mix-ups. *Toddler Talk*. https://toddlertalk.com/blog?offset=1685015700086

Kirby, J.R., & Bowers, P.N. (2017). Morphological instruction and literacy. In: K. Cain, D.L. Compton, & R.K. Parrila (Eds.), *Theories of reading development* (pp. 437–488). John Benjamins. https://doi.org/10.1075/swll.15

Kirby, J.R., Deacon, S.H., Bowers, P.N., Izenberg, L., Wade-Woolley, L., & Parrila, R. (2012). Children's morphological awareness and reading ability. *Reading and Writing*, *25*, 389–410.

Lowry, L. (2018). "He's combining words…now what??!" Helping children develop early sentences. *Hanen Early Language Program*. https://www.hanen.org/SiteAssets/Articles---Printer-Friendly/Research-in-your-Daily-Work/Helping-children-develop-early-sentences-PF.aspx

Lowry, L. (2016). *Early sentences: A big step in language development*. The Hanen Centre. https://www.hanen.org/Helpful-Info/Articles/Early-Sentences-%E2%80%94-A-Big-Step-in-Language-Developme.aspx

Mackay, E., Lynch, E., Sorenson Duncan, T., & Deacon, S.H. (2021). Informing the science of reading: Students' awareness of sentence-level information is important for reading comprehension. *Reading Research Quarterly*, *56*, S221–S230.

Torcasio, S., & Sweller, J. (2010). The use of illustrations when learning to read: A cognitive load theory approach. *Applied Cognitive Psychology*, *24*(5), 659–672. doi: 10.1002/acp.1577

5

The Sounds of Language

Phonological and Phonemic Awareness

Playing with speech sounds happens when we chant rhymes with our toddlers, sing silly songs with our preschoolers, or clap the number of syllables in our names with our kindergarteners. Through these relatively simple auditory activities, children begin to recognize that spoken words are made up of smaller component parts. Those individual sound parts might be words, syllables, onsets, rimes, or phonemes, and when children begin to demonstrate their *phonological awareness*, an awareness of the phonological structure of words, they are building a foundation for reading and writing (Ehri et al., 2001; Ehri, 2023; Olson, 1990). When I taught kindergarten, I always found these types of games, songs, and rhymes to be effective and quite amusing for the children I taught. Silly sound attendance, for instance, engaged the children to tune into the initial sound of each child's name. By replacing the initial sound of each child's name with a letter-sound that we might have been focusing on that day, children were given the opportunity to practise their phonological skills. If we were focusing on the /b/[1] sound, for example, Clare would become Bare, Jamie would become Bamie, and Oscar would become Boscar. It was also an efficient way to check in on whether a child could in fact hear and manipulate initial sounds.

DOI: 10.4324/9781032688558-5

Monitoring a child's phonological skills by playing simple games like silly song attendance can provide a quick and formative assessment to help identify a child's strengths and any areas that might need more targeted instruction, and of course, these silly songs were hilarious to most of the four- and five-year-olds I taught. We would often play this game or a variation of it. For instance, when lining up for outdoor play I would sing "Willougby Wallaby Woo" by Canadian poet Dennis Lee (1974). When the children heard the alternative version of their name, they would jump up and get into line. The poem goes like this:

Willougby wallaby woo, an elephant sat on you.
Willougby wallaby wee, an elephant sat on me.
Willougby wallaby Wonnor (pause), an elephant sat on Connor.
Willougby wallaby Welanie (pause), an elephant sat on Melanie.

If the children could identify initial sounds in words, they would usually jump up at the nonsense name that started with /w/ before even hearing their actual name.

Phonological awareness involves the ability to notice, think about, and manipulate sounds in spoken words (Torgesen & Mathes, 1998). There are two main aspects related to the acquisition of phonological awareness: Learning that words can be divided into segments of sound and learning that the smallest units of sounds in words are *phonemes* (Torgesen & Mathes, 1998). Children who develop strong phonological awareness skills are better prepared for reading since understanding that speech sounds can be divided into smaller sounds helps children "break the code" of written language and acquire the alphabetic principle, which can be described as "recognizing that printed words comprise letters and that these letters correspond to sounds heard when the word is read aloud" (Piasta, 2023, p. 83). Conversely, children who have difficulties learning to read often have core deficits in phonological skills (Lyon et al., 2003; Wagner et al., 1997). Given the substantial amount of research showing a causal relationship between early skills in phonological awareness and later reading achievement (Del Campo et al., 2015; Hogan et al., 2005; Wagner & Torgesen, 1987), it is essential for children to have opportunities to develop these skills even before they begin formal school.

Levels of phonological awareness

Phonological awareness can be thought of as an umbrella term, with words, syllables, onsets and rimes, and phonemes as subcategories (The National Center on Improving Literacy (2022) has created a nice visual representation of the umbrella model: https://improvingliteracy.org/). Figure 5.1 shows the levels of phonological awareness and how the complexity of each activity increases with each subcategory.

At the simplest level, *the word level*, a child might show their phonological awareness skills through rhyming. You might ask a child to tell you a word that rhymes with *cat*, or perhaps you tell a child new to this activity that the word *cat* rhymes with *bat*. From there, you could ask the child to tell you other words that rhyme with *cat* and *bat*. Alliterations can also occur at the word level in which the first sound of each word in a phrase or sentence is the same (e.g., "Big brown bear" is an alliteration since all the words begin with the sound /b/). Children can also show and practice their phonological skills at the word level by

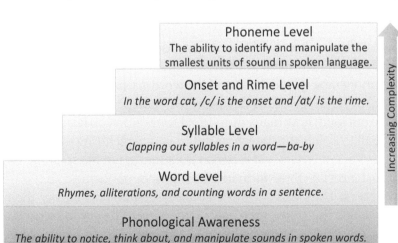

FIGURE 5.1 Levels of phonological awareness.

breaking apart and counting the number of words in a sentence, as in the sentence "I see a brown dog" = five words.

At the next level of phonological awareness, *the syllable level*, a child might be able to break apart or segment syllables in a word by clapping out each syllable: ba-by has two syllables and ex-er-cise has three syllables. As a parent or teacher in an early childhood environment, you might ask a child or group of children to say the word *bookcase* and then say it again but don't say *book*. A child who says *case* is demonstrating their ability to identify and manipulate syllables in words.

Playing with onsets and rimes in words has also shown to positively influence a child's phonological skills (National Institute of Child Health and Human Development, 2000). An *onset* is the initial phonological unit of any word that is part of the syllable and precedes the vowel (/c/ is the onset in the word *cat*). The term *rime* refers to the string of letters that follow the onset; rimes are usually composed of a vowel and final consonant(s) (/at/ is the rime in *cat*). Take a more complex word, like *stamp*. Here the onset is the blend, /st/ and the rime is /amp/. Knowing about onsets and rimes can help children learn about word families, which can lay the foundation for future spelling strategies.

The most difficult level associated with phonological awareness is the *phoneme level*. Phonemes are the smallest unit of sound in spoken language, and developing *phonemic awareness* means that you can identify and manipulate phonemes (Kilpatrick, 2020). In English there are about 44 phonemes, depending on dialect. Most words in English have at least two phonemes: The word *it* uses two phonemes: /i/ and /t/, and the word *dog* has three phonemes: /d/, /o/, and /g/. Consider your own name: When you say your name out loud, how many individual sounds do you hear? It can be difficult to isolate the speech sounds if you're picturing the spelling of the word, so try to just focus on the sounds, not the spelling. *Eli*, for instance, has three individual sounds, or phonemes: /ē/,[2] /l/, and /ī/. If I say each of those sounds separately, then say them again a little bit faster, then again even faster, I'll start to blend the sounds together to eventually make the word *Eli*.

Where *Eli* has three letters and three distinct sounds, words in English are rarely composed of the equal number of letters and sounds. Different letter combinations might only produce one sound and some letters in words are silent. Take the name *Jane*, which is composed of four letters; however, you only hear three sounds /j/, /ā /, and /n/. The letter *e* is silent and takes on the role of making *a* say its long vowel sound or its own name. Another example is the name *Jamie*. When you say this name aloud, you hear four sounds, even though the name is composed of five letters; when combined, the *i* and *e* make one sound, the /ē / sound.

Researchers agree that effective phonemic awareness instruction teaches children to notice, think about, and manipulate sounds in spoken language (National Institute of Child Health and Human Development, 2000). While many children develop phonemic awareness implicitly, direct and explicit instruction in phonemic awareness can build children's understanding and awareness of phonemes and is especially important for some children. Building an understanding that spoken language is composed of phonemes directly relates to learning to read (Ehri et al., 2001; National Institute of Child Health and Human Development, 2000). In fact, research has shown that phonemic awareness is a very important independent predictor of early reading outcomes; developing phonemic awareness is seen as a precursor to skilled reading (e.g., Anthony et al., 2007; Wagner & Torgesen, 1987). Developing phonemic awareness can be challenging for a lot of children and is especially difficult for some children who might have phonological processing deficits (Adams et al., 1998). This is why it is critically important to help children develop phonemic awareness before and while they learn the letter names and *graphemes* (the written representation of phonemes). It might be difficult for us, as adults and fluent readers, to think about, say, or listen to the sounds in words without also thinking about the corresponding graphemes. When thinking about the sounds in a word, I find it challenging, for instance, to say the word *cat* without picturing the spelling of *cat*. However, for young children at the earliest stage of reading development (the pre-alphabetic phase), playing with just the sounds in words can, and does, occur without needing to know any of the letters that represent them (Smith et al., 1998). Of course, once you begin introducing graphemes, children are still building their phonemic awareness skills. At the same time, they begin applying their skills to reading and spelling words (Adams, 1990).

With almost twice as many sounds as there are letters (26 letters in English) it is easy to appreciate the fact that English is a rather opaque language. As we've seen with the above names (e.g., *Jane* and *Jamie*), English does not always have a one-to-one correspondence between the phonemes and graphemes, and letters in English can represent more than one sound. A one-to-one correspondence between the letter sounds and letter symbols does occur in other more transparent languages, like German and Finnish; learning to read either German or Finnish is relatively easier than learning to read English (Seymour et al., 2003). We'll get into greater detail about letter-sound associations and phonics instruction in Chapter 6. For now, let's continue with the foundational building block of phonemic awareness, where we're just dealing with the individual sounds in spoken language.

Simple phonemic awareness activities

Eight activities to support a child's development of phonemic awareness have been suggested by researchers, including the reading experts who formed the National Reading Panel and identified skills that should be included in every beginning reading programme (National Institute of Child Health and Human Development, 2000). Table 5.1 lists these activities, which increase in complexity and can be turned into simple games and formative assessments.[3]

Isolating phonemes into their individual sounds is the simplest type of activity to support children's development of phonemic awareness, especially when the sound being isolated is at the beginning of a word (the initial sound). You might ask a child to isolate the first sound in a word, like /d/ in *dog*. In this case, a child is also *identifying phonemes* in words. An increasingly complex activity for identifying phonemes could be recognizing that the final sound is the same in the words: *bus*, *house*, and *miss*. When a child *categorizes phonemes*, they sort words according to the sounds they

TABLE 5.1 Activities to support phonemic awareness

Activity	Description
Phoneme Isolation	Isolating each phoneme or individual sound in a word. The word dog has three sounds, /d/ /o/ /g/.
Phoneme Identity	Identifying each individual sound in a word. The last sound in the words *bus, miss*, and *house* is /s/.
Phoneme Categorization	Sorting words according to the sounds they hear and don't hear. Which word does not belong? – *bug, ball*, and *mat*
Phoneme Blending	Combing individual sounds to make words. /h/ /a/ /t/ is *hat*
Phoneme Segmentation	Breaking apart words into individual sound units. How many sounds are in the word *cup*? /c/ /u/ /p/
Phoneme Deletion	Deleting individual sounds to create new words. The word *smile* is *mile* without the /s/.
Phoneme Addition	Adding individual sounds to make a new word. What word do you have if you add /s/ to the beginning of park? *spark*
Phoneme Substitution	Changing sounds in a word to make a new word. The word is bug. Change /g/ to /n/. What's the new word? *bun*

hear and don't hear. For example, a child might identify the word that has a different initial sound in a group of words, like *bug, ball*, and *mat*. A simple game that provides practice with identifying and categorizing phonemes is Sound Bins. This game involves a group of about ten different small objects and two small bins or baskets. Most of the objects should have the same initial sound. For instance, if the initial sound you want children to identify and categorize is /b/, you might have the following small objects and toys (or images) ready to be drawn from a bag: ball, banana, bead, bug, bus. The other objects can either all be unrelated or be a group of objects based on a second sound. After a child draws an object from the bag, they say the name of the object aloud and listen for the initial sound. Once the child identifies the initial sound, the child decides which bin or basket to put the object into, based on whether the sound is /b/, as in this case, or not.

Grasping these relatively simple activities leads to skills in *blending phonemes*. Blending sounds to make words is the beginning of reading words. Combining the phonemes /h/ /a/ /t/, for instance, to make the word *hat*, might involve a game where the adult says each individual sound after which the child blends the sounds to say the word (keep in mind that we're still just dealing with the sounds in language and not necessarily applying phonemic awareness by associating these sounds with the symbol that represents their sound—more on this soon). At the same time as blending sounds, children can begin to *segment phonemes* by breaking apart words into individual sound units. Take the word *cup*. An adult might ask a child to listen for the individual sounds in the word *cup*. A child who has developed their phonemic awareness skills will be able to say each individual phoneme, /c/ /u/ /p/. Gestures and materials can be used and manipulated while children practise blending and segmenting the sounds they hear in words. Have children move their hands apart and "stretch out" sounds to hear each individual phoneme. Slinkies are also a great tool to use while "stretching out" words.

Deleting phonemes from words, *adding phonemes* to words, and *substituting phonemes* in words are more complex activities (and are related to onsets and rimes, as in the earlier examples). For instance, a child might delete phonemes to recognize that the word *smile* is *mile* without the /s/ (as the parent or teacher you could ask the child to say the word *smile*, then say it again but this time without the /s/). Similarly, adding phonemes to make a new word might occur when a child is asked to add /s/, for instance, to the word *park* making the word *spark*. Finally, an effective activity to support a child's development of phonemic awareness involves *substituting phonemes*, as in the silly song attendance game I described earlier; changing the /c/ to a /b/ in the name *Camryn* you get *Bamryn* involves manipulating the smallest units of sounds in words and allows a child to practise their phonemic awareness skills.

From the field: Articulate!

While these are indeed effective and research-based activities, and playing games involving phoneme blending, segmenting, and so on will improve a child's phonemic awareness skills, it's almost just as important to ensure that you, the parent or teacher, are truly isolating the individual sounds. Take the sound /f/, for instance, and say it aloud to yourself. You might notice the shape of your mouth and where the air is flowing. As you make the sound /f/, your top teeth should be on top of your bottom lip and the sound should be continuous (you can keep vocalizing the sound until you run out of breath). If you find that your mouth opens after saying /f/, then you're likely producing two sounds and not actually isolating the individual sound, /f/. Do you hear a short /u/ at the end, as in /fu/? If so, you might be vocalizing /f/ and a short /u/. This can sometimes be confusing for someone who is just beginning to understand and identify the individual sounds in the English language. For this reason alone, it is critically important to practise articulating each of the 44 sounds in English so that the sounds are individually represented.

In talking to teachers through my research, I've heard them comment on the production of phonemes and how for some of them there was a moment of realization during a professional development activity that helped them understand the importance of truly isolating each individual sound in a word. The manner of articulation is the "how" of making speech sounds. When we speak, a combination of airflow, contracting muscles, and the shape and position of our tongue, lips, and mouth helps us produce the 44 distinct sounds in English. Take the sound /f/ and now add its counterpart, /v/, to the mix. Say each sound out loud, and as you say each sound hold your hand to your throat. As you vocalize /v/, you should feel a vibration happening, whereas a vibration doesn't happen when you produce /f/. This is because when producing /v/, your vocal cords are vibrating. This type of speech sound is known as a *voiced* consonant phoneme. Making the sound /f/, on the other hand, doesn't cause a vibration and is hence a *voiceless* consonant phoneme. To get even more technical /v/ and /f/ are known as *fricatives* since the airflow is continuous (*fricatives* occur when you can continuously produce the sound until you run out of breath).

Consonant phonemes that do not run on and on are known as *stops* and include /b/ (which is voiced) and /p/ (which is voiceless). Both /b/ and /p/ are produced with the same mouth position, the difference is just whether the vocal cords are vibrating or not. Other dimensions of articulation include *nasals, affricatives, liquids*, and *glides* (Moats, 2020). As the term implies, *nasals* (which are just three consonant sounds in English: /m/, /n/, and /ng/ as in *sing*) are produced through the nose, which differ from all other consonant sounds which can be described as *oral sounds*, since the air flows through the mouth rather than the nose. *Affricatives*, like /ch/ as in *chin* and /j/ as in *jug*, are a combination of a closed stop and then immediate release of air (try saying /ch/ slowly and take note of the change in the position of your mouth as you say the sound). There are just two *liquids* in English, /r/ and /l/, which are the most challenging for a child to learn since they are known to "float" in the mouth (Moats, 2020); there isn't really a beginning or ending placement of a liquid sound. You might notice a toddler pronouncing /l/ or /r/ differently. The word *squirrel*, for instance, can be tricky for a two-year-old to properly articulate and can sound more like *sklirlel*. Finally, *glides* are known to have vowel-like qualities and include /w/ as in *went* and /y/ as in *yes*. Glides are always followed by a vowel. When /w/ and /y/ are found at the end of a word, like in *snow* and *toy*, they are not actually being represented as glides, but rather they work with the previous vowel as a vowel pairing or vowel team (Moats, 2020). Vowel sounds in English are produced with a vocal fold vibration and, therefore, are voiced phonemes. What changes the most for vowel sounds is the tongue's position and shape (for a good list of vowel sound articulations see Moats, 2020).

Of course, as fluent speakers we don't spend time or energy thinking through the process of producing each sound we make, how the mouth is formed, and whether we are contracting our vocal folds (although perhaps this could be a good way to practise isolating each individual phoneme!). When introducing speech sounds to our beginning learners, however, it is critically important to pay attention to what is happening with your breath, vocal tract, mouth, lips, and tongue. Practising these sounds in front of a mirror can be helpful (for children, teachers, and parents too!). A fantastic video from the website Reading Rockets shows the mouth formation for each of the 44 English speech sounds and is a good resource for someone new to the idea of attending to and isolating the smallest sounds in speech (https://www.youtube.com/watch?v=wBuA589kfMg&t=118s). While articulating speech sounds is something that happens almost automatically when children first learn to isolate phonemes, ensuring that students attend to the articulation of speech can be especially helpful for individuals with language-related weaknesses (Hogan et al., 2005). You can also use Figure 5.2 as a reference guide for the 44 sounds of English. We'll learn in the next chapter on phonics that there are sometimes multiple ways to represent one sound.

The main goal of teaching phonological and phonemic awareness skills is for children to develop an understanding and awareness of the sounds we hear in spoken language. Children with strong phonological and phonemic awareness skills have the tools they need to begin to read and spell words. Helping students apply their phonemic awareness skills to reading and spelling words by connecting the sounds of English with the printed symbols that represent those sounds is the next step in "breaking the code." It's important to keep in mind that we do not want to withhold decoding instruction until phonemic awareness fully develops. Consider Ehri's second phase of word reading, the *partial alphabetic phase*. Children at this phase have made connections between some of the letters in written words and sounds detected in their pronunciations (Ehri, 2023). As such, children at this phase can indeed begin to read and spell some words, based

Vowel Sounds	ee *feet*	ĭ *ship*	oo *book*	oo *moon*	ai *wait*	oa *boat*		
	ĕ *fed*	er *teacher*	ir *bird*	or *horse*	our *tourist*	oy *toy*	ow *cow*	
	ă *cat*	ŭ *hug*	ar *star*	ŏ *dog*	ĭ *itch*	i *bike*	air *fair*	
Consonant Sounds	p *pat*	b *bug*	t *toad*	d *dog*	ch *chase*	j *jar*	k *kite*	g *go*
	f *fan*	v *vote*	th *think*	th *that*	s *see*	z *zoo*	sh *sheep*	s *envision*
	m *mice*	n *nest*	ng *sing*	h *hat*	l *love*	r *race*	w *went*	y *yak*

FIGURE 5.2 The 44 sounds of spoken English.

on the letter-sounds they have learned. Phonics is the instruction that teaches children the letter-sound associations and is the main topic of Chapter 6.

Tips for supporting phonological and phonemic awareness

♦ Count out words in a sentence or syllables in a word.
♦ Drum out syllables of children's names or other identified words.
♦ Isolate sounds by using a robot-like voice.
♦ Sing rhyming songs like *Down by the Bay* and *Row, Row, Row the Boat* (change the first sound in "Row").
♦ Read books with rhyming patterns and have children say aloud the upcoming rhyming word.
♦ Focus on one sound at a time.
♦ Use gestures and materials to blend and segment sounds.
♦ Practise isolating individual phonemes by observing your mouth formation in a mirror.
♦ Use a PVC elbow joint to create a rotary-like "phoneme phone." Listen while you blend and segment sounds in words.
♦ Use counting chips or another manipulative to help isolate sounds in words.

Recommended books for supporting phonological and phonemic awareness

♦ *Alligator Pie* by Dennis Lee
♦ *Brown Bear, Brown Bear, What Do You See?* by Eric Carle
♦ *Each Peach Pear Plum* by Allan Ahlberg
♦ *Fox in Socks* by Dr Seuss
♦ *Goodnight, Goodnight Construction Site* by Sherri Duskey Rinker
♦ *Rumble in the Jungle* by Giles Andreae
♦ *Sheep in a Jeep* by Nancy Shaw
♦ *The Snail and the Whale* by Julia Donaldson
♦ *Wemberly Worried* by Kevin Henkes
♦ *Zin! Zin! Zin! A Violin* by Llloyd Moss

Notes

1 As pointed out in Chapter 2, the double backslash is used to represent the sound of the letter as opposed to the letter name.
2 A straight line above a vowel (called a macron) indicates the long vowel sound, whereas a curved line (called a breve) indicates the short vowel sound.
3 Formative assessments are done to monitor a child's learning and provide ongoing feedback. They can also be used by teachers (and parents) to better target an area that needs improvement.

References

Adams, M. J. (1990). *Beginning to read. Thinking and learning about print.* MIT Press.

Adams, M., Foorman, B., Lundberg, I., & Beeler, T. (1998). *Phonemic awareness in young children.* Baltimore: Brookes.

Anthony, J.L., Williams, J.M., McDonald, R., & Francis, D.J. (2007). Phonological processing and emergent literacy in younger and older preschool children. *Annals of Dyslexia, 57,* 113–137. https://doi.org/10.1007/s11881-007-0008-8

Del Campo, R., Buchanan, W.R., Abbott, R.D., & Berninger, V.W. (2015). Levels of phonology related to reading and writing in middle childhood. *Reading and Writing, 28*(2), 183–198. https://doi.org/10.1007/s11145-014-9520-5

Ehri, L.C., Nunes, S.R., Willows, D.M., Schuster, B.V., Yaghoub-Zadeh, Z., & Shanahan, T. (2001). Phonemic awareness instruction helps children learn to read: Evidence from the National Reading Panel's meta-analysis. *Reading Research Quarterly, 36*(3), 250–287.

Ehri, L.C. (2023). Phases of development in learning to read and spell words. *American Educator, 47*(3), 17–18. https://files.eric.ed.gov/fulltext/EJ1394529.pdf

Hogan, T.P., Catts, H.W., & Little, T.D. (2005). The relationship between phonological awareness and reading: Implications for the assessment of phonological awareness. *Language, Speech, and Hearing*

Services in Schools, *36*(4), 285–293. https://doi.org/10.1044/0161-1461(2005/029)

Kilpatrick, D.A. (2020). *Equipped for reading success: A comprehensive, step-by-step program for developing phoneme awareness and fluent word recognition*. Casey & Kirsch Publishers.

Lee, D. (1974). *Alligator pie*. Macmillan Publishers of Canada.

Moats, L.C. (2020). *Speech to print: Language essentials for teachers*, (3rd ed.). Paul H. Brookes Publishing Co.

National Center on Improving Literacy. (2022). *Phonological awareness: What is it and how does it relate to phonemic awareness*. Washington, DC: U.S. Department of Education, Office of Elementary and Secondary Education, Office of Special Education Programs, National Center on Improving Literacy. http://improvingliteracy.org.

National Institute of Child Health and Human Development. (2000). *Report of the National Reading Panel—Teaching children to read: An evidence-based assessment of the scientific research literature on reading and its implications for reading instruction* (NIH Publication No. 00-4769). Washington, DC: U.S. Government Printing Office.

Lyon, G.R., Shaywitz, S.E., & Shaywitz, B.A. (2003). A definition of dyslexia. *Annals of Dyslexia, 53*, 1–14.

Olson, M.W. (1990). Phonemic awareness and reading achievement (research into practice). *Reading Psychology, 11*(4), 347–353.

Piasta, S.B. (2023). The science of early alphabet instruction. In S.Q. Cabell, S.B. Neuman, & N.P. Terry (Eds.), *Handbook on the science of early literacy* (pp. 83–94). Guilford Publications.

Seymour, P.H., Aro, M., Erskine, J.M., & Collaboration with COST Action A8 Network. (2003). Foundation literacy acquisition in European orthographies. *British Journal of Psychology, 94*(2), 143–174. https://doi.org/10.1348/000712603321661859

Smith, S.B., Simmons, D.C., & Kameenui, E.J. (1998). Phonological awareness: Research bases. *What reading research tells us about children with diverse learning needs: Bases and basics* (pp. 61–127). Routledge.

Torgesen, J.K., & Mathes, P.G. (1998). *What every teacher should know about phonological awareness*. Florida Department of Education, Division of Schools and Community Education, Bureau of Instructional

Support and Community Services. https://www.fullertonsd.org/cms/lib/CA50010905/Centricity/Domain/1993/PA-_what_you_should_know_.pdf

Wagner, R.K., & Torgesen, J.K. (1987). The nature of phonological processing and its causal role in the acquisition of reading skills. *Psychological Bulletin*, *101*(2), 192–212. https://doi.org/10.1037/0033-2909.101.2.192

Wagner, R.K., Torgesen, J.K., Rashotte, C.A., Hecht, S.A., Barker, T.A., Burgess, S.R., … & Garon, T. (1997). Changing relations between phonological processing abilities and word-level reading as children develop from beginning to skilled readers: A 5-year longitudinal study. *Developmental Psychology*, *33*(3), 468. https://psycnet.apa.org/buy/1997-06205-008

6

"The Cat Sat"

Alphabet Knowledge and Phonics

When I taught kindergarten, the programme I used for teaching the letter-sound relationships took a systematic and explicit approach. It was systematic in that the letters and letter-sounds were introduced in an order that followed a carefully planned scope and sequence and increased in complexity; it was explicit in that the letter names and sounds were stated clearly with direct reference to the corresponding symbols. A set of five or six letter sounds and associated letters or letter combinations would be introduced throughout the course of several days so that the children I taught could begin *decoding* (blending sounds together to read words) and *encoding* (listening to the letter-sound relationships to spell words) right away, before they had even learned all the letter-sounds of English and the letters or combination of letters that represent them. The first set in the scope and sequence I followed was /s/, /t/, /a/, /p/, /i/, and /n/ (Jolly Learning, 2024). Each *grapheme* (the written letters and letter combinations that represent each of the 44 sounds in English) would be shown to the children and the name and sound it made would be shared. Take the letter *s*, for instance. I would usually write the lowercase letter on the white board stationed in our gathering place, and as I wrote the letter I would state, "this is the letter *s*, the letter *s* makes a /s/ sound." The children would repeat and recite

DOI: 10.4324/9781032688558-6

the letter sound through chants, rhymes, and songs, as well as write the letter on a whiteboard or with their finger in the air. We would then brainstorm words that included the letter *s*. I would ask, "Can you think of a word that begins with /s/?" This kind of question was always met with eager hands waving in front of me. We would listen to each child say their word and as they reported their word, I would add it to the list. We usually started with the initial sound, and in subsequent days, we would also brainstorm words that had the same sound in the middle or at the end of a word. If a child gave a word that didn't include the targeted sound, I would ask the group to listen carefully for the sound as I stretched out the word. The child who might have initially given this word would nod in agreement that they didn't hear the targeted sound after all, and if there was any confusion, I would make a mental note to check in again with this same child later that day. Introducing and playing games with the grapheme-phoneme correspondences would often happen with the whole class in short periods (about 10 minutes). However, I would also work with smaller groups to really target instruction, especially since the children entering kindergarten came in with a range of skills, with a few children already blending and reading simple words. The small targeted group instruction allowed me to work with three or four children who were at the same place in the scope and sequence.

Blending two or three of the letter-sounds from the set of six would happen rather quickly for most children, who would begin to read and spell simple words, usually following a CVC pattern (CVC = consonant-vowel-consonant, like *sat* or *sip*). You can probably think of quite a few words that use a combination of the first set of letters and letter-sounds I would introduce— sit, tip, pin, it, in, pants, paint… When the children I taught started reading and spelling words, they were always eager to learn more; beginning to learn to read, even just few words, is a motivator in itself. Of course, this phonics routine was just one part of my literacy programme, balanced with the other key components of effective literacy instruction that should be part of every beginning reading programme (phonemic awareness, vocabulary, fluency, morphology, reading comprehension). But it was a significant component, to say the least, and a component that researchers agree should be included in every beginning reading programme (National Institute of Child Health and Human Development, 2000; Lonigan & Shanahan, 2009; Rand & Morrow, 2021; Snow, 2017).

Phonics instruction (for alphabetic languages, like English) has been around for decades, centuries really, beginning with "hornbooks," single-sided alphabet tablets used as early as the late 1600s as a primer for learning the English alphabet (Barry, 2008). The main goal of phonics instruction is to help children learn the alphabetic principle, the idea that there are visual symbols (letters or graphemes) that represent the sounds of spoken language; the alphabet is a code and breaking the code involves learning to read (Chard & Osborn, 1999). Teaching the letter-sound relationships for reading and spelling in a systematic and explicit way is an important component of any beginning reading programme, the research on this is clear. Yet at times, phonics instruction has been a contentious topic (Semingson & Kerns, 2021). Phonics does not make up an entire literacy programme, and it does not just mean monotonous drills and memorization. Effective phonics instruction provides frequent opportunities for children to apply their knowledge of letters and sounds to the reading of words, sentences, and longer phrases. These opportunities can occur through chants, rhymes, songs, and games, beginning with parents at home before children enter kindergarten.

The process of learning the letter-sound (grapheme-phoneme) relationships provides children with an understanding that graphemes map onto speech in predictable ways (Moats, 2020). As I'll discuss in Chapter 10, *Reading in Cars: Motivation for Literacy*, this process can be empowering for beginning readers. David Share proposed the idea that once children have established an understanding of letter-sound relationships (and how to blend and segment to read and spell words), they begin to apply this understanding to new unfamiliar words (1995). Each time a child comes across an unfamiliar word, they can apply their knowledge of phonological decoding (using the sounds they know to decode the word). This leads to *orthographic mapping*, the cognitive process by which children learn to read words by sight and to spell words from memory which allows children to automatically recognize words and read increasingly complex texts (Ehri, 2014). Share describes this as a "self-teaching" mechanism; readers become independent and autonomous decoders which can be highly motivating for literacy learning (1995).

Teaching phonics: Instruction in letter-sound relationships

There are about 250 graphemes (letters or letter combinations) in English which indeed implies many combinations of letters and sometimes several ways to spell one sound (Moats, 2020). For instance, *digraphs* occur when two letters combine to make one sound, like /th/, /sh/, /ch/, and /ng/. These are consonant digraphs, whereas /ea/, /oo/, and /ai/ are examples of vowel digraphs. Another phonics term to keep in mind is *diphthong*, which can be thought of as a gliding vowel where two vowel sounds glide together in one syllable. Examples of diphthongs are /ow/ as in *cow* and /oy/ as in *toy*. When introducing graphemes, you'd likely begin with single grapheme-phoneme or letter-sound correspondences at a rate of about two to four letter-sound relationships each week (University of Florida Literacy Institute [UFLI], n.d.). It might also be helpful to teach the voiced /th/ sound since the word *the* shows up quite a bit in beginning texts. Additionally, it's important to consider that in English there can be a combination of multiple graphemes that make just one sound. For instance, four graphemes like -ough as in the word *though* or -eigh as in the word *sleigh* make a single long vowel sound (-ough = /ō/, -eigh = /ā/). These types of spellings would show up much later in a scope and sequence since they are considered low-frequency spellings. It is important to note that explicit and systematic phonics instruction is good for all children and students, and especially important for some children and students, like those with reading difficulties or disabilities such as dyslexia. A scope and sequence a kindergarten or grade one teacher (or parent) could use includes the following concepts, in this order (UFLI, n.d.):

1. Consonant and Short Vowels (e.g., m /m/,[1] s /s/, a /ā/)
2. Consonant Digraphs (e.g., sh /sh/, ck /ck/, ng /ng/)
3. VCe (vowel-consonant and final silent e; e.g., a_e /ā/, i_e /ī/)
4. R-Controlled Vowels (e.g., ar /ar/, er /er/)
5. Vowel Digraphs (e.g., ea /ē/, ee /ē/, ai /ā/)
6. Diphthongs (e.g., oy /oy/, oi /oi/)
7. Silent letters (e.g., kn /n/, mb /m/)
8. Low-Frequency Spellings (e.g., ough /ō/, eigh /ā/)

Teaching about types of written syllables is also something to consider in a phonics programme (Knight-McKenna, 2008). Moats (2020) suggests that knowing syllable types is useful because they help children recognize and recall longer printed words more efficiently since they indicate vowel sounds in syllables. They also help explain spelling patterns such as doubled letters. There are six basic types of spelling patterns for syllables (Moats, 2020):

1. Closed: a syllable with a short vowel, spelled with one letter, ending in one or more consonants (e.g., pen, sun, fish).
2. Vowel-Consonant-*e*: A syllable with a long vowel spelled with one vowel, one consonant, and a final silent *e* (e.g., cape, rope, fine).
3. Open: A syllable that ends with a long vowel sound, spelled with a single vowel letter (e.g., she, hi, piano).
4. Vowel team: Syllables with long, short, or diphthong vowel sounds that use a letter combination for spelling (e.g., dr**ea**m, b**ou**nce, b**oa**t).
5. Vowel-*r*: A syllable with a single vowel letter followed by r (*ar, er, ur, ar, ir*); an r-controlled vowel (e.g., sh**ar**p, tig**er**, b**ir**d).
6. Consonant-*le*: An unaccented final syllable containing a single consonant, *l*, and silent *e* (e.g., bubb**le**, spectac**le**, pur**ple**).

There are many patterns that are not included in this list, especially those patterns that come at the end of words (suffixes). Examples include *-ive, -age, -ion*.

When teaching the alphabetic principle and letter-sound relationships, it can be important to introduce the lowercase letters first and to focus on the letter sounds; although this doesn't mean that you ignore uppercase letters, especially if printing is part of your literacy programme—learning to print capital letters before lowercase letters is often the sequence of a handwriting programme. The main reason for emphasizing lowercase letters is that most words that we read are indeed written in lowercase and we read the sounds of the letters not the letter names. Approaching phonics in this way gives beginning readers a greater chance of success when reading their first books. These first books, known as *decodable* books, can be available to children right away to help them build their confidence in reading. Decodable books are short and simple books that include the letter-sound correspondences the children have learned. They provide children with practice applying their alphabetic knowledge to decode or sound out new words. Sentences you might find in a decodable book include:

♦ *The cat sat.*
♦ *Pat is a cat.*
♦ *The dog is on the log.*

In a review of existing studies examining decodable books, Cheatham and Allor (2012) found decodability to be an important component of early reading texts since decodability increases the likelihood that students will use decoding as a strategy to read unfamiliar words. Applying decoding skills to read new words also results in immediate benefits, particularly regarding accuracy. Cheatham and Allor (2012) also highlight the need for students to apply phonics skills in connected text and suggest that decodable text positively impacts early reading progress. A comprehensive list of decodable texts has been created by The Reading League and includes decodable books for primary students and older students (up to grade 8!) (https://www.thereadingleague.

org/decodable-text-sources/). Along with introducing decodable books, children can apply their alphabet knowledge through simple games and activities. Here are five examples of simple phonics games and activities you can try out at home or in the classroom.

Alphabet scavenger hunt

Place letter cards around a room. Show pictures of animals and objects and ask the children what sound they hear at the beginning of the word. For instance, if you show a picture card of a tiger, children would identify the initial sound /t/; if the picture card is a chimpanzee, then children would identify the initial sound /ch/. Once the letter-sound has been identified, have children look around the room for the letter (or letter combination, as in /ch/) that matches the initial sound. The letter or grapheme cards can be placed around the room prior to the start of the game.

Mystery bag

Place a handful of letters into a bag (consider including letters that you can combine into simple words). Have children pull out one letter at a time. As they pull out each letter, encourage the child to say the letter name and letter sound. Have them make simple consonant-vowel-consonant (CVC) words with the letters they pull from the bag.

Fishing for phonics

Using a toy fishing pole or net (or even a large spoon), have children "fish" for letters from a water-filled container. You can use foam or plastic letters and as each letter is pulled out of the container, the name of the letter and the letter-sound can be said aloud.

Alphabet soup

Put magnetic or wooden letters (or letter cards) into a bowl. Using a large soup spoon or ladle have children scoop out letters as they say each letter name and sound. You can also have the children build simple words with the letters they scoop out of the bowl.

Drive-thru blending

This is a great activity for blending sounds together to make words. Start with three letter cards and place each one about a hand-width apart. Using a toy car, have children drive the car past each letter card while saying each letter sound. Children can move their cars faster as they drive through each sound until they read the word.

Understanding the alphabetic principle to build decoding and encoding skills is just one area of literacy and the amount of time that a teacher should spend on phonics instruction depends on a child's stage of reading development. As I mentioned in Chapter 1, Linnea Ehri wrote about the phases of reading and how the proportion of time spent on reading components changes as children move from one phase to the next (1999; 2023). Dale Willows has also written about the phases of literacy development and provides informative visuals to show the proportion of skills that should be emphasized at each phase or stage of literacy development (Ontario Institute for Studies in Education, 2021). Those at stage three, for instance, have built strong foundational reading skills in phonemic awareness, letter-sound associations, fluency, and vocabulary, so that they are able to read to learn new ideas, gain new knowledge, and learn about new perspectives. It's at around the beginning phases of reading (Willows uses "stage 0" to designate the earliest stage, which is in line with Ehri's phase one) that children begin to learn about how the English writing system works.

It's important to think about phonics and decoding as just one of the steps, albeit an important step, to breaking the code and becoming a fluent reader (see Figure 6.1 for a visual representation of the steps to breaking the code). Having phonological and phonemic awareness as well as a strong understanding of letters, letter combinations, and their sounds contributes to a child's ability to apply their knowledge of letter-sound relationships to read and spell unfamiliar words, and ultimately, to be

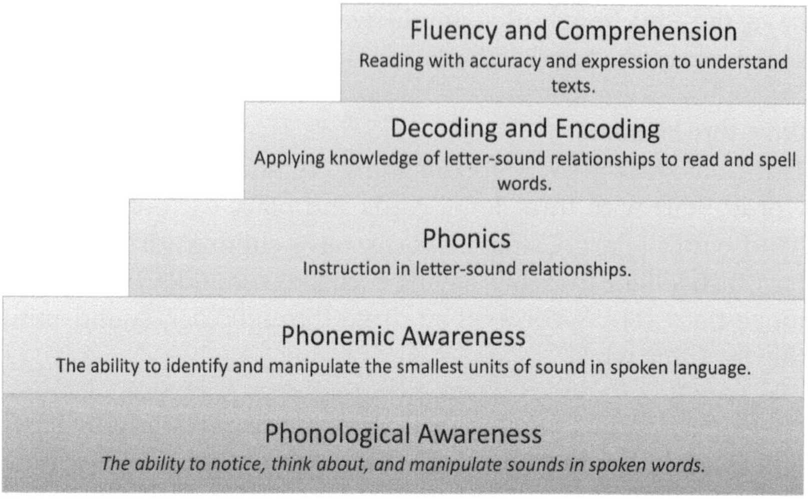

Fluency and Comprehension
Reading with accuracy and expression to understand texts.

Decoding and Encoding
Applying knowledge of letter-sound relationships to read and spell words.

Phonics
Instruction in letter-sound relationships.

Phonemic Awareness
The ability to identify and manipulate the smallest units of sound in spoken language.

Phonological Awareness
The ability to notice, think about, and manipulate sounds in spoken words.

FIGURE 6.1 Steps to breaking the code.

able to automatically recognize words and read with fluency and accuracy. Fluent readers can spend their cognitive resources on comprehending and thinking critically about what they are reading (more about reading fluency in Chapter 7).

As much as there should be an emphasis on phonics instruction in the early grades or phases of reading, this emphasis shouldn't neglect language-related skills, like critical thinking while reading and developing critical literacy, vocabulary, and background knowledge. The report from the National Reading Panel advised that daily phonics instruction shouldn't be more than 30 minutes (National Institute of Child Health and Human Development, 2000). The rest of the language programme and how language is embedded across subjects should provide ample opportunities to not only practise word-level reading skills but also to support the development of language-related skills, like pointing out new vocabulary words and discussing their meanings in science or social studies. This balance between print and language-related skills, like vocabulary, background knowledge, and reading comprehension, was certainly the case during my school visits and in my conversations with teachers.

From the field: Phonics instruction in the Montessori context

When I first walked into a Montessori school in the fall of 2022, I found myself surrounded by children scattered around the room on rolled-out mats completely immersed in their work. One child sat very focused at a table with one of the teachers, practising his printing skills. The other children used a variety of learning materials like number rods, sandpaper letters, and knobbed cylinders while they engaged in sensorial, mathematics, and language activities. This was my first visit to a Montessori classroom, and my expectations were certainly met, and even exceeded by what I observed and in discussion with the teachers. Our conversations and my tour of the classroom, in which the language and literacy-related materials and programme were highlighted, led me to a more comprehensive understanding of how literacy, and specifically the letter-sound relationships and phonics, are taught and learned in a Montessori context.

Like my other classroom experiences, literacy development in this (and any) Montessori classroom is rooted in a language-rich environment. This is something that Maria Montessori certainly advocated for in her schools (Feez, 2009). At this particular Montessori school, print was all around the room and accessible to the children, the teachers were engaged in several conversations with children individually and in small groups, and the materials that the children were using were associated with language, either directly related to print or a language-related skill like vocabulary. In any Montessori classroom, children begin building onto their language skills with games and lessons associated with phonological and phonemic awareness. "I Spy" is one lesson in which the children find an object that begins with the target sound. A teacher might say, for instance, "I spy, with my little eye, something that begins with /c/." The child then finds an object in the room that begins with this sound. Pretty simple and straightforward, and a game that we all likely know and have played at some point in our lives. Yet, as discussed in the previous chapter on phonological and phonemic awareness, this type of game provides children with opportunities to play with the sounds of English and builds a necessary foundation for phonics. Once a child has begun to associate phonemes with the corresponding letter or combination of letters, they start putting the letters together to create and write words. The Montessori teachers consistently refer to the letter symbols by the sounds they make, so the children learn the sounds before they learn the letter names, which, as I've described, makes sense given that the goal of this phase of word-level reading is to blend and segment the sounds in written words (not the letter names).

In a Montessori classroom, the process of blending sounds together to read and spell words is indeed a systematic and explicit process. It is also a multisensory one. Reading and writing are visual, auditory, and tactile activities in a Montessori environment. Take the Sandpaper Letters activity, for instance. As children say the sound of the letter, they feel the shape of the letter by tracing the letter in sand with their fingers. The Moveable Alphabet also allows the children in a Montessori classroom to touch, feel, and work with wooden letters to make words. The tactile and multisensory experience can be engaging and a focus for children's attention. The order in which the letter-sounds are introduced is also systematic allowing the children to begin to read and spell words right away.

These print-based activities are done in conjunction with other language-related activities, like building vocabulary and oral language skills with read alouds, storytelling, and speaking during circle time (or any time of the day!). All these experiences certainly coincide with *the simple view of reading*, where reading comprehension is a product of *both* decoding and language-related skills. The conversations I had with teachers across contexts indicated how dedicated and reflective they are in their language and literacy planning and instruction, and how their own learning about best practices continues to grow. On one hand, the teachers I spoke with understood the importance of being explicit and using structured literacy so that skills are taught in a systematic way. These same teachers described how language and literacy can be fostered across subject areas and in language-rich environments, and how a literacy programme must be based upon what the research says about teaching literacy. Several components of literacy, including oral language, phonemic awareness, phonics, vocabulary, morphology, fluency, and reading comprehension, must be included in any beginning literacy programme (National Institute of Child Health and Human Development, 2000).

Tips for teaching phonics

♦ Be explicit and introduce the letter-sound correspondences in a systematic order.
♦ Incorporate games, rhymes, and chants into your phonics instruction.
♦ Use actions, gestures, visuals, and tactile material as letter names and sounds are taught and practiced.
♦ Provide instruction to both whole groups and small groups.
♦ Let children read and spell words with the letter-sound associations they've been taught.
♦ Create your own sentences that include the letter-sound correspondences you've taught.
♦ Start with the lowercase letters.
♦ Focus on the letter sounds.
♦ Start with consonant-vowel (CV) or consonant-vowel-consonant (CVC) words when beginning to blend letter-sounds together to read and spell words (e.g., me, sat).

Recommended books for supporting alphabet knowledge

♦ *Bob Books* by Bobby Lynn Maslen
♦ *Bubblegum Delicious* by Dennis Lee
♦ *Cat on a Mat* by Brian Wildsmith
♦ *Cat the Cat Who Is That?* by Mo Willems
♦ *Click, Clack, Moo* by Doreen Cronin
♦ *Green Eggs and Ham* by Dr Seuss
♦ *Llama Llama Red Pajama* by Anna Dewdney
♦ *The Cat in the Hat* by Dr Seuss
♦ *The Flea's Sneeze* by Henry Holt

Note

1 The first letter indicates the letter name, whereas the second is the letter-sound.

References

Barry, A. (2008). Reading the past: Historical antecedents to contemporary reading methods and materials. *Reading Horizons: A Journal of Literacy and Language Arts, 49*(1), 31–52.

Chard, D. J., & Osborn, J. (1999). Phonics and word recognition instruction in early reading programs: Guidelines for accessibility. *Learning Disabilities Research & Practice, 14*(2), 107–117. DOI: https://doi.org/10.1007/s11145-011-9355-2

Cheatham, J. P., & Allor, J. H. (2012). The influence of decodability in early reading text on reading achievement: A review of the evidence. *Reading and Writing, 25*, 2223–2246.

Ehri, L.C. (1999). Phases of development in learning to read words. In J. Oakhill & R. Beard (Eds.), *Reading development and the teaching of reading: A psychological perspective* (pp. 79–108). Blackwell Science.

Ehri, L. (2014). Orthographic mapping in the acquisition of sight word reading, spelling memory, and vocabulary learning. *Scientific Studies of Reading, 18*, 5–21. doi: 10.1080/10888438.2013.819356

Ehri, L.C. (2023). Phases of development in learning to read and spell words. *American Educator, 47*(3), 17–18. https://files.eric.ed.gov/fulltext/EJ1394529.pdf

Feez, S. (2009) *Montessori and early childhood: A guide for students*. Sage Publications.

Jolly Learning. (2024). *Jolly Phonics*. https://www.jollylearning.co.uk/

Lonigan, C.J., & Shanahan, T. (2009). *Executive summary: Developing early literacy: Report of the National Early Literacy Panel*. Washington, DC: National Institute for Literacy. https://files.eric.ed.gov/fulltext/ED508381.pdf

Knight-McKenna, M. (2008). Syllable types: A strategy for reading multisyllabic words. *Teaching Exceptional Children, 40*(3), 18–24.

Moats, L. C. (2020). *Speech to print: Language essentials for teachers* (3rd edition). Paul H. Brookes Publishing Co.

National Institute of Child Health and Human Development. (2000). *Report of the National Reading Panel—Teaching children to read: An evidence-based assessment of the scientific research literature on reading and its implications for reading instruction* (NIH Publication No. 00-4769). Washington, DC: U.S. Government Printing Office.

Ontario Institute for Studies in Education. (2021). *The Stages of Literacy Development.* https://www.theliteracybug.com/stages-of-literacy

Rand, M.K., & Morrow, L.M. (2021). The contribution of play experiences in early literacy: Expanding the science of reading. *Reading Research Quarterly*, *56*(S1), S239–S248. https://doi.org/10.1002/rrq.383

Semingson, P., & Kerns, W. (2021). Where is the evidence? Looking back to Jeanne Chall and enduring debates about the science of reading. *Reading Research Quarterly*, *56*, S157–S169. https://doi.org/10.1002/rrq.405

Share, D.L. (1995). Phonological recoding and self-teaching: Sine qua non of reading acquisition. *Cognition*, *55*(2), 151–218. https://doi.org/10.1016/0010-0277(94)00645-2

Snow, C.E. (2017). Early literacy development and instruction: An overview. In N. Kucirkova, C. E. Snow, V. Grøver, & C. McBride-Chang (Eds.), *The Routledge international handbook of early literacy education: A contemporary guide to literacy teaching and interventions in a global context*, (pp. 5–13). Routledge.

University of Florida Literacy Institute. (n.d.). *UFLI Foundations.* https://ufli.education.ufl.edu/foundations/

7

Meaning Makers

Reading Fluency and Comprehension

Literature circles were part of my students' literacy learning when I taught grade three. Small groups of four or five students would meet regularly to talk about a book they were all reading. Their conversations would revolve around the plot, characters, themes, connections, inferences, and vocabulary of a chapter book they chose from a given selection. Guided by prompts and question sheets, the literature circles provided the students with an opportunity to read a text with purpose. Literature circles were formed based on the students' interests and choice, and not every group read the same book (book selection also depended on the library copies—we needed to ensure that there were at least four copies of each book, including audio book options, to form a productive group). For each chapter or selected section of the book, each student would take on a role: The *Questioner* would think of relevant questions, like why did this character act in this way? The *Connector* made connections to the book, based on other books, personal experiences, or world events. Someone would also take on the role of the *Word Wizard* and select and explain new and interesting words from the chapter. The *Illustrator's* job was to share a visual interpretation of the selected chapter. Sometimes we would also have a *Discussion Director*, *Summarizer*, and *Literacy Luminary*. Taking on this last

DOI: 10.4324/9781032688558-7

role meant finding important sections or quotes to read and discuss. These roles would rotate through the group members so that over the course of several meetings, students would be responsible for contributing to the discussion in different ways. Much like an adult version of a book club, our literature circles encouraged thoughtful discussion, engagement in reading, and a deeper understanding of the text.

The goal of reading is to make meaning from text and media in our world, whether through the books we read, signs we see on the streets, or recipes we follow from the backs of cereal boxes. Making meaning from text is empowering and can open doors to new perspectives and information. The literacy components discussed in the previous chapters include language-related and print-related skills, all of which set a foundation for "breaking the code" of the English alphabet and making meaning from text. As beginning readers apply foundational skills to reading words, they enter the *consolidated alphabetic phase* (Ehri, 1999, 2023). Letter sounds and patterns that recur across different words become consolidated and readers begin to automatically recognize words by sight and read with fluency, phrasing, and expression. Fluent readers can then spend their cognitive resources on comprehending, synthesizing, and analysing text, rather than on blending letter-sounds together to decode individual words. Fluent readers can read for depth by paying careful attention to details and using a variety of strategies to gain a deeper understanding of the text's messages.

Reading fluency

Reading fluency is one of the defining features of reading texts and involves three key elements: accuracy, rate, and prosody (see Figure 7.1; Hudson et al., 2005).

Attention to each of these component parts leads to accurate word reading at a conversational rate and with appropriate expression. Fluent readers automatically read most words, which allows them to move away from frequent pauses to solve unknown words towards more rapid word reading with

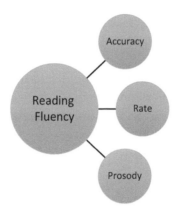

FIGURE 7.1 Elements of reading fluency.

fewer pauses. Word reading accuracy stems from a beginning reader's ability to decode words using their knowledge of the alphabetic principle and letter-sound relationships (Ehri, 2023). As discussed in Chapter 6, effective instruction in phonics can help beginning readers build the necessary foundational skills in blending sounds together to read words, sentences, and longer phrases. As automaticity increases, so too does an individual's reading rate. The rate at which someone reads should be at a conversational speed, not too fast or too slow. Reading too fast or too slow could decrease the likelihood of focusing on the words and hence the meaning of the text. Readers who read too fast might move through the text too quickly to make any sense of what they are reading. On the other hand, a pace that is too slow might indicate word-by-word phrasing and more effortful decoding.

Accurate reading at an appropriate pace is only one part of the fluency picture. Fluent readers also move away from monotone phrasing towards a more natural rise and fall in pitch, tone, and rhythm, where there is greater attention to punctuation and text form. *Prosody* is a linguistic term used to describe the rhythmic and tonal aspects of speech; it can be thought of as the "music" of oral language (Dowhower, 1991; Hudson et al., 2005). Prosodic reading occurs when a reader varies their pitch (intonation), stress (loudness), and duration (timing); a prosodic reader segments the text into meaningful units marked by appropriate pauses, varied duration of those pauses, the rising and lowering of pitch, lengthening of vowel sounds, and emphasis of certain words (Dowhower, 1991). Reading with these prosodic features can enhance text comprehension, particularly when the meaning is drawn from one of these features, like a stressed word in a given sentence. For example, when reading the question, "are you really tired?" the meaning can change depending on the inflection given to the word "really." The question could refer to being very tired, where there is a neutral emphasis on the word "really" or genuinely tired, where there is a heavy emphasis on the word "really" (this example comes from Bolden & Beach, 2021). When individuals read with fluency AND prosody, they actively engage with the text. This type of intentional reading also provides evidence that a reader *understands* what they are reading.

Fluent reading allows us to attend to the meaning of the text since cognitive resources become more available for comprehension (NICHD, 2000). All children can benefit from fluency practice and for some children, this practice is critical (Moats, 2009). A well-researched approach to reading fluency instruction is *repeated oral reading* (Rasinski, 1990; Washburn, 2022). Repeated oral reading is exactly how it sounds; children read aloud the same text multiple times until it is read with fluency and prosody. A child can focus on a particular aspect of reading fluency each time the text is read. For instance, for their first reading of a text, a child might work on reading accuracy, ensuring that each word is read correctly. The rate at which the text is read can be the next area of focus, where the child who can now read all the words accurately, is attending to the rate or pace at which they read. Along with rate, a child might add prosodic elements during subsequent readings, like changes in pitch.

Fluency practice and repeated oral reading

Repeated oral reading begins with modelled reading, where the elements of fluency are modelled and discussed. Shared reading experiences at home and in the classroom are perfect opportunities to model fluent reading. When I taught at the primary level, I would sometimes ask the children in my class to focus on a particular element of fluency as I read a text or passage aloud. This type of modelled instruction would be especially engaging if I did the opposite of what a fluent reader should sound like. Reading too quickly and with no expression would immediately be met with eager voices pointing out the problems. A follow-up discussion would ensure that the children understood the key aspects of reading fluency. Partner reading, radio reading, and reader's theatre were three instructional techniques I incorporated into my teaching practice. Each involved repeated oral readings of the same text.

Partner reading

In partner reading, pairs of either the same reading ability or different abilities meet to read a text together. Encouraging the pair to sit elbow-to-elbow and knee-to-knee can provide a shared reading experience where the book sits between the children who sit side-by-side. As one child reads a section aloud, the second listens in and follows along. Ensuring that the children understand the story premise or key elements of the text can occur with question prompts the listener can ask after the reader has completed the passage. Partner reading could also happen at home, between siblings or between a parent and child. As you and your child sit side-by-side have your child read aloud while you focus on accuracy, rate, and expression. If your child misreads a word, for instance, give them a moment to catch their error and self-correct. However, if they carry on and continue reading, consider going back to the misread word before turning to the next page or after the book has finished, depending on the book's length and your child's motivation. When looking at the word again, guide your child in using their decoding skills to sound out the word. Use your finger to follow along as each sound is read aloud. If your child still struggles to read the word, it's okay to tell them what the word says. You can even read it slowly at first, repeating each sound separately before blending the sounds together to read the word. Make a mental note to find opportunities to practise reading and spelling this word or other words with similar spelling patterns. As you and your child engage in shared or partner reading, talk about the other elements of fluency before and after reading and don't hesitate to pick up the same book on multiple occasions. With each reading, you should begin to hear your child's fluency increase to an appropriate rate and with greater expression.

Radio reading

Radio reading is the second instructional strategy I incorporated into my teaching practice and can certainly be an activity that a primary or junior-level teacher can implement in the classroom or that a parent can practise with their child at home. Radio reading begins with reading through a new piece of text, either a text the child has selected or one that they have written themselves. Once the child feels comfortable with the selected text, their voices are recorded as they read through the passage, as though they are broadcasting a news story or recording a podcast. The recording is then played back while the child listens in and considers elements of fluency that they would like to practise. Listening to a recording of yourself for the first time can sound a bit strange, but once you get used to the idea that your voice sounds a bit different when it's played back to you, radio reading can be highly successful and might even turn into an entire news hour, podcast series, or audio book.

Reader's theatre

Reader's theatre is another approach that can be helpful for engaging children in repeated reading exercises. The main premise of reader's theatre is for pairs or small groups to read through a script several times (three or four, for instance), each time paying attention to a feature of reading fluency (see Figure 7.1). Each group member takes on a role (or two) of a character from a selected script. On the first read through, you might have the children read their lines to themselves, highlighting their sections as they read. The second reading can involve all group members reading through their lines together. In subsequent readings, the children are likely to begin reading their lines at an appropriate rate and with increased prosody and expression, especially if you, the teacher or parent, act like a coach and provide direct feedback to the children as they engage in their readings.

The goal of reader's theatre is to provide opportunities for oral reading fluency practice, not to memorize a script and perform in front of an audience, like you might expect of an extra-curricular drama club. Of course, if there is interest in a performance, the group can feel encouraged by keeping their script with them and reading their lines during the performance. But the performative aspect of reader's theatre isn't necessary and should only be secondary to the fluency practice.

Additional strategies for parents or teachers to use with their children to practise reading fluency include listening to audio books or online stories. Just like reading aloud to your child, audio books and online stories provide opportunities to hear fluent readers. *Fluency phones*, which are pieces of PVC elbow pipes connected to form a telephone shape, can also be highly effective. When children read into a fluency phone (think of a rotary phone that has a curved handle rather than a flat smartphone), their voice, even when it's just a whisper voice, is amplified by the shape of the phone. This provides opportunities to focus on and attend to the various elements of reading fluency, including rate and prosody.

Figure 7.2 shows fluency as the bridge between decoding and comprehension. At one end, fluency connects to accuracy and automaticity in decoding. At the other end, fluency connects to comprehension through prosody and interpretation. When someone reads a text accurately, with an appropriate rate, and attends to prosodic features, they are better able to understand the text being read. As I've mentioned at the beginning of this chapter and elsewhere in the book, the purpose of reading is to

FIGURE 7.2 Reading fluency: The bridge between decoding and comprehension.

make meaning from text. *The simple view of reading* asserts that reading comprehension occurs when an individual has skills in both print-related and language-related components. As a result of applying both sets of skills, the text laid out in front of an individual can be read with fluency and comprehension.

Reading comprehension

Reading comprehension can be defined as "intentional thinking during which meaning is constructed through interactions between the text and reader…it's the construction of meaning of a written text through a reciprocal interchange of ideas between the reader and the message in a particular text" (NICHD, 2000, p. 4–39). Constructing meaning and comprehending text can happen because cognitive resources aren't exhausted with the basic skills of decoding. Deep rather than surface-level or passive reading is a goal of constructing meaning and comprehending text. Deep level processing during reading requires a reader to be strategic and use metacognitive and higher-level comprehension skills or strategies, as well as activate prior knowledge and be motivated to read.

Strategic reading

Reading comprehension involves the act of being metacognitive, the ability to monitor your thinking; to know when and why to do what (McKeown & Beck, 2009). *Metacognition* is an internal process that allows proficient readers to be strategic while reading. Before reading, a proficient reader might clarify the purpose for reading and preview the text; after reading, a proficient reader might check their understanding by summarizing the main points. Learning about which strategies to use and practising them can provide children with a greater awareness of the strategies they should apply before, during, and after reading to better understand what they are reading. There are several strategies or tools that can be learned and applied, including monitoring our understanding (or misunderstanding) of a given text. When we monitor our learning during reading, we can realize when a problem arises or when the text is not understood. Comprehension monitoring instruction teaches individuals to be aware of what they do understand, identify what they do not understand, and use appropriate strategies to resolve problems in comprehension (Armbruster et al., 2001). Armbruster et al. (2001) recommend the following strategies for monitoring comprehension (p. 42):

1. Identify where the difficulty occurs (e.g., "I don't understand the second paragraph on page 76.").
2. Identify what the difficulty is (e.g., "I don't get what the author means when she says, 'Arriving in America was a milestone in my grandmother's life.").
3. Restate the difficult sentence or passage in their own words (e.g., "Oh, so the author means that coming to America was a very important event in her grandmother's life.").
4. Look back through the text (e.g., "The author talked about this character in Chapter 2, but I don't remember much about him. Maybe if I reread that chapter, I can figure out why he's acting this way now.").
5. Look forward in the text for information that might help them to resolve the difficulty (e.g., "The text says, 'The groundwater may form a stream or pond or create a wetland. People can also bring groundwater to the surface.' Hmm, I don't understand how people can do that...Oh, the next section is called 'Wells.' I'll read this section to see if it tells how they do it.").

Along with monitoring comprehension while reading, strategic comprehension can be enhanced by using graphic organizers, answering questions, generating questions, recognizing text structure, summarizing (retelling), and inferring (see Figure 7.3; Armbruster et al., 2001). These comprehension strategies engage the reader to actively make a conscious plan to understand the text. Research has shown that explicit instruction in these

FIGURE 7.3 Components of strategic comprehension.

strategies can be effective for better understanding a given text and reading for depth (Moats, 2009). Explicit comprehension instruction involves stating exactly what strategies to use and how to apply them (Armbruster et al., 2001). Activities can be adapted for home or the classroom.

Using graphic organizers

Venn diagrams, story maps, and storyboards are types of *graphic organizers* that can help readers focus on concepts and interrelationships among concepts in a text (Armbruster et al., 2001). Semantic organizers or "webs" are also a type of graphic organizer that puts the central concept at the centre (see Figure 3.2 from Chapter 3 for an example of a graphic organizer). Other related concepts are connected to the central concept through connected lines, somewhat like a spider web. In general, graphic organizers help readers focus on the text structure as they read, particularly when reading a non-fiction text, provide readers with a visual representation of the relationships in the text, and help individuals when organizing information for a written summary or synopsis.

Answering questions

When readers are tasked with *answering questions*, they are better able to guide and monitor their learning (McKeown & Beck, 2009). Questions related to a given text can be effective for improving learning from reading because they give a reader a purpose for reading, focus attention on what is being learned, and provide opportunities for active thinking while reading (Armbruster et al., 2001). Types of questions that a teacher or parent might ask before, during, or after reading a text or selected passage might be either "on-the-page" questions or "off-the-page" questions. *On-the-page questions* involve information directly connected to the text and require no further action than simply retelling what is written in the text. These "right there" questions ask readers to find one correct answer located in the text. Examples of on-the-page questions are "What vehicle did the main character use to get to the city?" and "Did the main character play on the swing or the slide at the park?" *Off-the-page questions*, on the other hand, are more open ended and require readers to combine their prior knowledge and own experiences with what they have learned from reading the text. This can be referred to as inferential thinking, where the reader chooses the most likely explanation or conclusion based on prior knowledge, experience, and information from the text. Rather than the information being directly on the page, information is implied and not directly stated in the text. It's where the expression, "read between the lines" comes from. Examples of "off-the-page" questions are "How might the main character feel if they decide to move to a different city?" and "What do you think the author hoped you would learn after reading the text?"

Generating questions

Generating questions before, during, and after reading has been shown to increase a reader's engagement with the text and contribute to a deeper understanding of what is being read (NICHD, 2000). Like when we apply any of these strategies, generating questions improves a reader's active processing of text and comprehension (NICHD, 2000). Before, during, or after reading, a reader can write their own questions about important information or facts from the text, which in some ways is also monitoring comprehension. If a reader, for instance, pauses before even opening a book, and asks, "I wonder why the author decided to give the story this title?" they are already taking an active role by being on the lookout for the answer to this question. Providing children with opportunities to generate questions could involve Post-it notes, where questions are composed on the Post-it note and inserted directly into the text. A child could also be asked to come up with their own on-the-page and off-the-page questions before or after they read a given passage.

Recognizing text structure

Text structure is the way authors organize information and is based on text type or genre. The way a haiku poem is composed, for instance, might look quite different from an expository science text which could include headings, a glossary, and bolded fonts to highlight scientific vocabulary, features you wouldn't necessarily see in a haiku. Recognizing the structure of a text can help navigate key information within the text. When you pick up a story and know what story elements you'll encounter (e.g., plot, characters, problem, solution), you're likely priming yourself for understanding the text just by knowing the story structure. Signal words and other text features specific to a particular text structure can also improve comprehension (Wijekumar et al., 2014). Signal words you might find in a procedural text, for example, include *first*, *next*, *then*, and *finally*.

Summarizing

Summarizing or *retelling* is a synthesis of the important ideas in a text or what happens at the beginning, middle, and ending of a story. Retelling a simple story can happen with children as young as the toddler years. With question prompts like, "Can you tell me what happened first?" or "What happened at the end of the story?" a parent can encourage their toddler to share ideas about what has been presented in the text read aloud. Instruction in summarizing key ideas from a text in later years can help readers identify main ideas, connect central ideas, eliminate redundant information, and remember what they read (Armbruster et al., 2001).

Making inferences

Making inferences has also been shown to increase reading comprehension. Inferring requires a reader to draw conclusions by using
their prior knowledge and information stated in a text. The information from the text can be thought of as the evidence and helps
the reader make appropriate deductions, even if these deductions
are not directly stated and the reader needs to "read between the
lines" to figure out a character's intent, for instance. Helping children understand whether information is implied, as in "reading
between the lines," can improve inferential skills (NICHD, 2000).
In fact, we make inferences every day, not just when we read, and
building a child's confidence in knowing how to make an inference can lead to increases in self-efficacy for reading.

Marzano (2010, p. 80) suggests four questions parents and
teachers can pose to facilitate a discussion about inferences. The
first question, what is my inference? helps readers become aware
that they have just made an inference, which can happen automatically or with intent and based on available information. The
second question, "what information did I use to make this inference?" can make readers more aware of the evidence on which
their inference is based. "How good was my thinking?" is the
third question recommended by Marzano (2010) and involves
an examination of the validity of an inference or assumption.
The next question is Are there other possibilities or something
else that might happen? Guiding a reader by prompting them
to explain their thinking encourages a dialogue that can help the
reader further articulate their inference and whether it is indeed
believable, based on the given evidence. The last question is
"Do I need to change my thinking?" This final step in the process is for readers to consider whether their inference requires
modifications.

Making inferences can sometimes be quite abstract so it's
important to consider differentiated instruction. Images and video
clips can support learning as well as having students talk about
or draw, rather than write their inference. Graphic organizers can
certainly come into play here, where prompts and question starters, like the ones recommended by Marzano (2010), can be used
to help activate the process. It's also important to remember that
background knowledge varies, and the inference or conclusion

that a reader makes will be based on what the reader knows and their experience, or lack of experience with a given topic. Building background knowledge before reading a text, especially a domain-specific text, can help bridge any gaps in knowledge so that you, the parent or teacher, can get a true understanding of a child's inferential thinking and text comprehension.

Motivate!

We are motivated readers when we see a purpose and value in reading and take an active role. I'll discuss reading motivation in depth in Chapter 10, but for now it's important to connect motivation to comprehension. In particular, text difficulty can have a direct impact on a reader's motivation and hence their comprehension. If a text is too difficult, a reader might immediately turn away from the text or tune out and not focus on what they are reading. At the same time, a text that is too easy might also turn off a reader. A relatively easy text might not provide enough density for a reader to engage with the text and use higher-order processing skills. Thus, the reader only passively reads the text and isn't engaged in deep comprehension.

Fluent readers have built foundational skills in decoding and language comprehension and, as a result, they can read text with automaticity and prosody. This, in turn, contributes to their understanding of the text; a fluent reader can use their cognitive resources to understand, evaluate, synthesize, and critically examine text. Becoming a strategic reader is empowering and supporting our earliest readers with the tools they can use before, during, and after reading sets them up for success.

Tips for supporting reading fluency

♦ Provide practice through repeated oral reading exercises and activities.
♦ Have children focus on one element of reading at a time (e.g., rate).
♦ Some children find timed challenges fun and engaging; time a child as a passage is read aloud. Keep track of the times on repeated readings.

- Model the elements of reading during shared reading and include rate and prosody.
- Record, repeat, and reflect!

Tips for supporting reading comprehension
- Use a variety of graphic organizers.
- Have children ask questions before, during, and after reading a text.
- Include books in your book collection that include a variety of text structures.
- Have students summarize a story or retell the main ideas of a text.
- Activate and build students' background knowledge prior to reading a new text.
- Pre-teach new vocabulary.

Recommended books for supporting reading fluency and comprehension
- *Alexander and the Terrible, Horrible, No Good, Very Bad Day* by Judith Viorst
- *Benny The Bananasauras Rex* by Saraeth Holden
- *Charlotte's Web* by E.B. White
- *Cloudy with a Chance of Meatballs* by Judi Barrett
- *Malaika, Carnival Queen* by Nadia Hohn
- *Super Small* by Tiffany Stone
- *The Book with No Pictures* by B.J. Novak
- *The Kindest Red* by Ibtihaj Muhammad
- *Where the Wild Things Are* by Maurice Sendak

References

Armbruster, B.B., Lehr, F., Osborn, J., O'Rourke, R., Beck, I., Carnine, D., & Simmons, D. (2001). *Put reading first: The research building blocks for teaching children to read*. National Institute for Literacy, National Institute of Child Health and Human Development, US Department of Education. https://lincs.ed.gov/publications/pdf/PRFbooklet.pdf

Bolden, B., & Beach, P. (2021). Integrating music and literacy: Applying music concepts to support prosody and reading fluency. *General Music Today*, *3*(2), 5–12. https://doi.org/10.1177/1048371320926603

Dowhower, S. L. (1991). Speaking of prosody: Fluency's unattended bedfellow. *Theory Into Practice*, *30*(3), 165–175. https://doi.org/10.1080/00405849109543497

Ehri, L. C. (2023). Phases of development in learning to read and spell words. *American Educator*, *47*(3), 17–18. https://files.eric.ed.gov/fulltext/EJ1394529.pdf

Ehri, L. C. (1999). Phases of development in learning to read words. In J. Oakhill & R. Beard (Eds.), *Reading development and the teaching of reading: A psychological perspective* (pp. 79–108). Blackwell Science.

Hudson, R.F., Lane, H.B., & Pullen, P.C. (2005). Reading fluency assessment and instruction: What, why, and how? *The Reading Teacher*, *58*(8), 702–714. https://doi.org/10.1598/RT.58.8.1

Marzano, R.J. (2010). Teaching inference. *Educational Leadership*, *67*(7), 80–81.

McKeown, M., & Beck, I. (2009). The role of metacognition in understanding and supporting reading comprehension. In D. Hacker, J. Dunlosky, & A. Graesser (Eds.), *Handbook of metacognition in education* (pp. 7–25). Routledge.

Moats, L. (2009). Knowledge foundations for teaching reading and spelling. *Reading and Writing*, *22*, 379–399.

National Institute of Child Health and Human Development. [NICHD] (2000). *Report of the National Reading Panel. Teaching children to read: An evidence-based assessment of the scientific research literature on reading and its implications for reading instruction* (NIH Publication No. 00-4769). Washington, DC: U.S. Government Printing Office.

Rasinski, T. (1990). Effects of repeated reading and listening-while-reading on reading fluency. *The Journal of Educational Research*, *83*(3), 147–151. https://doi.org/10.1080/00220671.1990.10885946

Washburn, J. (2022). Reviewing evidence on the relations between oral reading fluency and reading comprehension for adolescents. *Journal of Learning Disabilities*, *55*(1), 22–42. https://doi.org/10.1177/00222194211045122

Wijekumar, K., Meyer, B.J.F., Lei, P.-W., Lin, Y., Johnson, L.A., Shurmatz, K., Spielvogel, J., Ray, M., & Cook, M. (2014). Improving reading comprehension for 5th grade readers in rural and suburban schools using web-based intelligent tutoring systems. *Journal of Research in Educational Effectiveness, 7*(4), 331–357. https://doi.org/10.1080/19345747.2013.853333

8

Mark Making

Letter Formation and Writing Development

At around the time that Eli turned 18 months, I noticed how he had started making, what seemed to be, more intentional marks with his crayons. Rather than grasping as many crayons in one hand as possible, which he still occasionally enjoyed doing, Eli's mark making began to show an early understanding that written language provides an avenue for expressing ideas. It also showed that he understood cause and effect—if I do this, then that happens. These marks were mostly lines formed across the entire area where the crayon seemed to barely leave the page, or they were more forceful staccato-like dots that resulted from Eli striking the page with the tip of the crayon. His pencil grasp looked like what you would typically expect from a toddler his age; a fully fisted grip, although he also held a crayon using a pronated grip which is the beginning of a more standard grip, just with the fingers pointed downwards and the whole arm doing the writing rather than finer movements at the wrist. Surprisingly at the time, Eli used a more standard finger-like tripod grip on several occasions. In any case, whether it was a meandering line or a palette of dots, Eli always seemed quite pleased with his creation.

Learning to form the letters of the alphabet (and any sign, symbol, or mark) begins with holding a writing utensil with a

DOI: 10.4324/9781032688558-8

full grasp and making randomly assorted marks, which you might call scribbling. Although there is always a range of skills and abilities to consider with any developmental sequence, children do, for the most part, pass through predictable stages of handwriting (e.g., Reading Rockets, 2024). As a child's fine motor skills develop, they begin to use a stronger grasp to draw and form letters and begin to make words. The importance of moving towards a more standard and adult-like tripod grip has to do with efficiency. It takes quite a bit of effort to write you name, for instance, with a fisted grip than with a tripod grip. Although I have seen a few kindergarten children write and draw beautifully with a fisted grip, guiding children towards a tripod grip (if needed) without influencing their motivation to write is important. The process can be tricky, but the magic can happen with the support of different tools, like a painting easel. If a child is asked to make marks or write their name on a piece of paper that has been set on an easel, then the child almost involuntarily rests the palm of their hand on the easel, almost like an anchor, which seems to automatically turn their grip into a tripod grip while they make their marks.

A developmental progression

The educational resource Reading Rockets (2024) shares a developmental progression of writing and spelling that begins with scribbling and moves towards more letter-like symbols (see Figure 8.1). Although the earliest scribbles do not resemble actual letters, as scribbles become more intentional (and as the child becomes more and more familiar with print in their environment because of adults pointing out print and directing the child to letters and words) some scribbles do in fact contain universal features of writing including directionality and linearity (Gombert & Fayol, 1992).

A child might progress through these early stages in the sequence outlined in Figure 8.1, but it's important to keep in mind, as with all stage-like models, that a child might not progress in a linear way. Flexibility with respect to the way in which

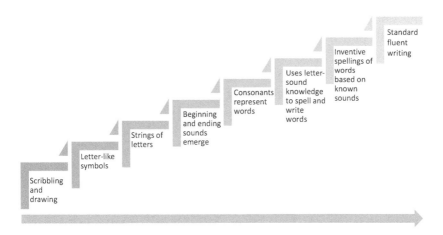

FIGURE 8.1 Developmental progression of spelling and writing.

a child might progress in their letter formation and spelling is key. Following random marks or scribbling, children might begin to string letters together—capital letters are usually easier to form at this early stage and spaces aren't always present. As a child begins to develop an understanding of letter-sound relationships (and as their fine motor skills develop), they start to represent words with the correct sound(s), at least the initial sounds. These more complex writing tasks require a more integrated knowledge system including knowing the letter-sounds and the symbols that represent them. Take this string of letters, for instance: BTRFLSORQT. Any thoughts about what this child is trying to express? Without spaces it's certainly difficult to decipher. But if the same child has drawn a picture of four butterflies in a row to go along with the string of letters, you might have a better chance at decoding the sentence. If spaces are added between the words, the string of letters would look like: BTR FLS OR QT which, if you haven't already guessed, can be decoded as *butterflies are cute*. This child has reached a stage in writing and spelling where they're able to use their phonemic awareness to encode or write words, expressing their ideas in writing. At first, initial sounds might be the only sounds of the words that are represented by print. The *butterflies are cute* example shows that the child is representing words with the initial and final sounds they hear in each word. This more proficient stage begins with the underlying mechanics of writing and the strengthening of a child's pencil grip. Their wrist stability, in-hand manipulation, fine motor skills, and posture all contribute to more efficient handwriting; when these mechanics are in place, a child can spend their energy *encoding* or writing words based on the sounds they know. Their cognitive load is decreased when handwriting is fluent and accurate (Graham et al., 2000).

From the field: Letter formation in Montessori classrooms

It was interesting to hear some of the teachers I talked to discuss letter formation as a precursor to fluent writing. They agreed that learning to form letters, either printed or cursive, is an essential step in the writing process. Handwriting was a regular focus and a skill the students in their classes practised daily. During a few of my Montessori school visits, I observed children practising their letter formations, using both print and cursive writing. In a Montessori school, this practice is usually done one-on-one with direct guidance from the teacher (Feez, 2009). Children will often use specifically designed materials; for instance, children might trace sandpaper letters or wooden letter blocks as they receive direct instruction on how to make marks and form letters. There is a basic progression towards becoming proficient in letter formation and handwriting, and as one of the teachers I met highlighted, with support from the teacher, children in a Montessori classroom would generally pass through each step sequentially. Children first work on strengthening the small muscles of their hand through games and activities that target fine motor skills. This might look like an infant or toddler playing with playdough or stacking blocks. Children around this age would also begin using specific materials that are designed to support a child's pencil grip. Knobbed cylinders, for instance, are shared with toddlers to help practise pencil grip and strengthen fine motor skills. Sandpaper letters are then introduced to children who begin to associate the letter-sounds to the shape of the letter. As children trace the sandpaper letters with two fingers, they are encouraged to say the sound aloud. When preschool children demonstrate a good pencil grasp, they progress to the metal insets to support their developing pencil control. Metal insets of various two-dimensional shapes are traced first on the inside of the inset, then on the outside. As children work with these materials they also freely draw, make marks, and form letters.

Benefits of making marks and forming letters

Letter formation and cursive writing are skills that have continuously been emphasized in Montessori schools since Maria Montessori first conceptualized the approach (Montessori, 1995). You might ask why letter formation and cursive writing are taught in the 21st century, in an era of digital technology and speech-to-text software. There are indeed benefits to learning how to form letters, both print and cursive. One benefit of learning how to write by hand relates to memory. Researchers argue that the process of expressing your ideas in writing, print or cursive, fires neurons related to memory which ultimately can have a positive impact on learning—when you take notes by hand you remember more of what you've written down than if you've typed it out (van der Meer & van der Weel, 2017). The process of writing by hand specifically integrates the sensory and motor areas of the brain due to the involvement of the senses as well as the fine and precisely controlled hand movements involved when writing by hand (Ose Askvik, van der Weel, & van der Meer, 2020). Memory and learning are thus boosted when notes are taken by hand as opposed to using a keyboard.

Handwriting has also been linked to letter processing which indeed underlies successful reading (James & Engelhardt, 2012). In a study that examined the brain functioning of five-year-old children who were given the task to either print, type, or trace letters, results suggested that learning to form letters by hand facilitated reading acquisition (James & Engelhardt, 2012). It's the experience of writing by hand and the relatively complex task of learning a specific series of strokes for each letter character, as well as the orientation of strokes, size, slant, and other smaller features of a letter that seem to activate the reading systems in the brain involved in letter processing (James & Engelhardt, 2012). Providing children with opportunities to practise making marks strengthens their fine motor skills and improves their ability to create these different strokes.

Developing fine motor skills

I've mentioned the term *fine motor skills* a few times now, so it's worth delving into more detail about what these skills entail. Fine motor skills are small hand muscle movements that require close hand-eye coordination and represent a skill set linked to handwriting (Bart, Hajami, & Bar-Haim, 2007; Luo et al., 2007). Strengthening the hand muscles involved in fine motor movements though is important for a range of activities, not just handwriting. For instance, think about the coordination involved when getting ready to go outside on a crisp November morning—zipping up your jacket, tying your shoes, wrapping your scarf around your neck, and so on. We seldom, if ever, stop to think about how our hands, fingers, and wrists move during a day-to-day activity, but if you do, you'd likely agree that these actions are indeed quite complex.

The muscles involved in fine motor skills can be strengthened by the act of handwriting itself, as well as through other types of games and activities, like manipulating small blocks or figures, threading beads, squeezing tweezers to pick up small pom poms, or playing with playdough and moulding clay. Other activities that can help strengthen fine motor skills (and ultimately improve pencil grip and handwriting) can be as simple as having your toddler peel off and place stickers onto a piece of paper or place coins in a piggy bank. Or, if your toddler is like Eli and thinks it's hilarious to grab the end of the toilet paper and run as fast as possible down the hallway to a place of solitude where he can start shredding the paper before being caught, then just know that you're giving your child an opportunity to strengthen their fine motor muscles. You can also give them an old magazine to rip out and scrunch up pages to throw across the room (another one of Eli's favourite activities but done with a box of tissue instead of a magazine).

Letter formation instruction

Given the link between handwriting, memory, learning, and early reading skills, it seems clear that opportunities to practise forming letters should be provided to children in the early years. In my own teaching experience, I've come across a few different handwriting programmes, which I've found to be relatively straightforward in terms of instruction and highly engaging for the children I taught. Like many handwriting programmes that can be used in the early years and primary grades, it's important that they take an explicit and systematic approach. Each lesson should directly teach a specific letter that the children practise forming in a particular way using given workbooks or copied pages. Letters should be introduced in groups of similar difficulty; for instance, introducing the letters L, F, E, H, T, and I in sequence would benefit children's learning since all these letters begin with the act of drawing a straight line in a downward motion. Likewise, the ways in which the letters are taught should consider multiple senses; children can use their finger to draw each letter in the air, they can be introduced to short rhymes and songs that coincide with how the letter is formed, and purposeful materials should be provided for guided practice, such as small chalkboards and chalk or wooden lines and curves. Olsen and Knapton (2008) suggest that children start with the uppercase letters, which are technically easier to form and potentially help with eliminating reversals. Studies have shown positive effects of using explicit and multisensory programmes, where children in grades one and two who used these types of handwriting programmes improved aspects of their handwriting, including spacing, size, and alignment (e.g., Marr & Dimeo, 2006; Roberts et al., 2014).

Moving beyond letter formation: Elements of writing

Skills in handwriting and letter formation are foundational to writing fluency. Along with capitalization and punctuation, skills in letter formation allow children to attend to higher-order aspects of writing; applying writing conventions effectively and efficiently creates opportunities to focus on spelling and grammar as well as more cognitively demanding elements of writing like planning, revising, and idea generation. Fluent writers are indeed aware of writing conventions; at the same time, they consider their audience and use clear and focused language to communicate their ideas. Besides the conventions of writing, elements of writing to consider including across kindergarten to junior-level classrooms include:

- Ideas: how the main themes and content are communicated.
- Organization: the internal structure of a piece of writing.
- Voice: the personal voice of the author in relation to the audience.
- Word choice: selecting words that are rich, interesting, and clearly communicate ideas.
- Sentence fluency: the flow of the writing, considering punctuation marks and rhythm.
- Presentation or text type: knowing the type of text and the formatting of the piece of writing can help communicate ideas more clearly.

These elements can be taught within the larger picture of the writing process, which usually begins with a prewriting strategy (e.g., creating an outline with key points), followed by a first draft, revisions, editing, and publishing. When I taught grade three, I would emphasize that this process was meant to be flexible. Not all writers follow this process rigidly; some might skip the prewriting strategy at first, for instance, but then go back and write a new outline or compose a concept map showing how new ideas will be connected in the next chapter. Sometimes my students would write a first draft or compose an outline and we'd leave it there. At times they would move through the entire process of writing, but this was something that we usually saved for a piece of writing that had some importance attached to it— where the students could maintain their motivation to write and see the piece of writing through to the publishing stage. Inviting guest authors to speak to your class, at any grade, can be informative for students to learn firsthand about the writing process.

Like reading, writing is a complex cognitive activity and isn't always straightforward. Hearing from an expert can put the writing process into a more realistic perspective.

I do, we do, you do

Key instructional approaches to writing, particularly when considering the higher-order aspects of writing, like ideas and voice, can follow a gradual release of responsibility framework. You can think of the framework as "I do, we do, you do," beginning with more directed demonstrations, moving towards more joint instruction where students collaborate on a piece of writing with the teacher, and finally having students apply the tools and strategies they've been taught directly during independent practice. *Modelled writing* is the first step in the framework, where a demonstration can show students specific aspects of writing. *Shared or interactive writing* can follow modelled writing, giving students an opportunity to collaborate on a piece of writing with considerable teacher support. This support is still available but less directed during *guided writing*; the teacher acts as a coach, providing feedback from the sidelines while students engage in the process. The goal of the gradual release of responsibility framework, of course, is to provide students with the tools, strategies, and practice to become successful *independent writers*. The cognitive work shifts from more teacher-directed instruction to more student-driven learning. These four approaches to teaching writing can involve any stage of the writing process (e.g., revising). Let's look at each—modelled, shared, guided, and independent—with specific examples.

Modelled writing

Modelling writing with a "write aloud" is an informative way to show your child or students that writing is a metacognitive process—we think about what we are writing while we write. During a "write aloud" you, the parent or teacher, would verbalize the internal dialogue you use as you write a particular type of text. By explicitly sharing the ideas that are running through your head while you write, your child or students can develop a greater awareness of the various elements of writing—they begin to self-monitor and question, as well as reflect on the purpose of their writing, the type of text, and perhaps even adjust their writing style for a particular audience. Individuals who are meta-cognitively aware while they write improve their understanding of these processes. As you describe your own decision-making process when it comes to the various elements (and conventions) of writing, you might say things like:

- I wonder if this introduction is catchy for my audience. Is there a more interesting word that I can use to help engage the reader?
- Hmm, I need to show that this character is excited. What should I have her say?
- Now that I am finished reading this chapter, I need to summarize the main points. I should go back to the outline I made and the notes I took while I read.
- Do I need a comma here or a semi-colon?
- What else should I include on this shopping list?

Modelling the writing process can be a good way to introduce a topic to your students and only requires a few minutes of whole class or small group instruction. Have your students practise reflecting on their thinking by recording their own questions and ideas as they write using Post-it notes—have them think of these notes as memos they can refer to at different points during the writing process. You might even have students purposefully stop at different time points during a writing task to reflect on the process.

Shared and interactive writing

Shared or interactive writing could involve a whole group lesson in which you and your child or students collaborate on a piece of writing using chart paper and markers or technology to which you might have access. One example of an interactive writing task I implemented with a primary class involved getting ready to go outside on a wintry day. The procedural or signal words, *first*, *then*, *next*, and *finally*, were introduced and discussed as the children and I brainstormed what we needed to do to get ready to go outside (besides being an engaging and effective writing task, this activity was also a good reminder to the children about how to get ready for outdoor play during the winter). Along with chart paper and markers, I would have my winter gear on standby (my winter jacket, toque, scarf, mittens, boots). I'd start by asking the children what I needed to put on first and how to go about doing this. I would demonstrate what the children would say, so any missed step, like putting your arms in the sleeves of the jacket, would often result in giggles and protests from the children. The demonstration would be followed by the written statement (something like: First, we put the jacket on our back. You put your left arm in the left sleeve…). To make it a truly interactive activity, a child would volunteer to write a word in the sentence or add a punctuation mark. While very much a demonstration, the process of writing the paragraph would be entirely student driven. The students were taking ownership of their writing with teacher support.

Guided writing

Guided writing involves small group instruction with groups of three or four children working together with the teacher after a whole group lesson in which a topic or activity has been introduced. The teacher acts as a coach providing immediate feedback and guidance as students engage in a short writing task (about 10 minutes). Guided writing can be viewed as the bridge between modelled and independent writing and can positively impact students' confidence in their writing skills. As a classroom teacher, I always found a guided writing task on revising to be especially impactful when working with small groups or one-on-one. Revising a piece of writing is different than editing, which mostly has to do with more surface-level aspects of writing like grammar, spelling, and sentence structure. Revisions delve deeper to reflect the higher-order elements of writing, like content, voice, word choice, and organization. Working at this deeper level often involves substantial modifications and challenging yourself, the writer, to view the piece of writing from different perspectives. For this reason, guiding students by providing them with direct and explicit feedback while they revise their work can be particularly effective.

Independent writing

Independent writing can occur at any stage in the writing process and doesn't need to involve a huge task of writing a complete narrative about a recent trip to the pumpkin patch, for instance. When I taught grade three, I would prompt my students in a "fast write" (which is a helpful strategy for any writer, at any stage of their writing development). During a fast write, students would be given a topic, or they would select a topic of their choice from a written list of ideas they had previously generated. The main objective of the fast write was to write freely in a very short amount of time (two to three minutes or so). To take the pressure off, I would emphasize that these fast writes weren't meant to be perfect and were more about getting ideas down on the page.

Supporting students' independent writing takes time and so, it's important to help students build their writing stamina by beginning with short writing tasks, like a fast write. Time on writing can increase regularly until students are writing independently for about 30–40 minutes. But time for writing isn't the entire picture. Setting clear and realistic goals for each writing task can help students monitor their time and progress. Familiar writing tools and resources (ones that you've demonstrated and had students practice using), like concept maps and story outlines, should be available to students as they write.

Building a solid foundation in letter formation and conventions leads to more fluent writers who have the tools to fully express their ideas in writing. As children are exposed to diverse texts and provided with daily opportunities to write, they begin to see themselves as writers and authors. This can be empowering and contributes to increases in self-confidence, independence, and becoming an effective communicator.

Tips for supporting letter formation and writing

♦ Support children's pencil grip with smaller-sized writing material and an easel.

♦ In lieu of a stand-up easel, use a binder to support children's developing pencil grip.

♦ Provide children with tactile materials when forming letters, like sandpaper and clay or playdough.

♦ Incorporate writing into play by placing writing materials in playhouses, kitchens, or any designated play area.

♦ Mazes and connect-the-dots are fun ways to help children strengthen their fine motor skills and pencil grip.

♦ Help children strengthen their fine motor skills by playing games with tweezers, stacking blocks, and threading beads.

♦ When teaching the elements of writing, focus on one at a time.

♦ Use picture books to model the elements of writing.

♦ Invite a local author to visit your class and talk about their writing process.

♦ Give children time to write every day!

Recommended children's books to support teaching the elements of writing

Idea generation:

♦ *Chester's Masterpiece* by Mélanie Watt
♦ *What Do You Do with an Idea?* by Kobi Yamada

Organization:

♦ *The Great Escape from City Zoo* by Tohby Riddle
♦ *The Mitten* by Jan Brett

Voice:

♦ *Diary of a Worm* by Doreen Cronin
♦ *Voices in the Park* by Anthony Browne

Word choice:

♦ *Brave Irene* by William Steig
♦ *The Keeper of Wild Words* by Brooke Smith

Sentence fluency:

♦ *The Great Kapok Tree* by Lynne Cherry
♦ *The Important Book* by Margaret Wise Brown

References

Bart, O., Hajami, D., & Bar-Haim, Y. (2007). Predicting school adjustment from motor abilities in kindergarten. *Infant and Child Development: An International Journal of Research and Practice*, *16*(6), 597–615. https://doi.org/10.1002/icd.514

Feez, S. (2009). *Montessori and early childhood: A guide for students*. Sage Publications.

Gombert, J.E., & Fayol, M. (1992). Writing in preliterate children. *Learning and Instruction*, *2*(1), 23–41. https://doi.org/10.1016/0959-4752(92)90003-5

Graham, S., Harris, K.R., & Troia, G.A. (2000). Self-regulated strategy development revisited: Teaching writing strategies to struggling writers. *Topics in Language Disorders*, *20*(4), 1–14.

James, K.H., & Engelhardt, L. (2012). The effects of handwriting experience on functional brain development in pre-literate children. *Trends in Neuroscience and Education*, *1*(1), 32–42.

Luo, Z., Jose, P.E., Huntsinger, C.S., & Pigott, T.D. (2007). Fine motor skills and mathematics achievement in East Asian American and European American kindergartners and first graders. *British Journal of Developmental Psychology*, *25*(4), 595–614. https://doi.org/10.1348/026151007X185329

Marr, D., & Dimeo, S.B. (2006). Outcomes associated with a summer handwriting course for elementary students. *The American Journal of Occupational Therapy*, *60*(1), 10–15. https://doi.org/10.5014/ajot.60.1.10

Montessori, M. (1995). *The absorbent mind*. Holt Paperbacks.

Olsen, J.Z., & Knapton, E.F. (2008). *Handwriting without tears pre-K teacher's guide*. Cabin John, MD: Handwriting Without Tears.

Ose Askvik, E., Van der Weel, F.R., & van der Meer, A.L. (2020). The importance of cursive handwriting over typewriting for learning in the classroom: A high-density EEG study of 12-year-old children and young adults. *Frontiers in Psychology*, *11*. https://doi.org/10.3389/fpsyg.2020.01810

Reading Rockets: Launching Young Readers. (2024). *Stages of Writing*. https://www.readingrockets.org/classroom/looking-writing/stages-writing

Roberts, G.I., Derkach-Ferguson, A.F., Siever, J.E., & Rose, M.S. (2014). An examination of the effectiveness of Handwriting Without Tears® instruction: Examen de l'efficacité du programme Handwriting Without Tears®. *Canadian Journal of Occupational Therapy*, *81*(2), 102–113. doi:10.1177/0008417414527065

van der Meer, A.L., & van der Weel, F.R. (2017). Only three fingers write, but the whole brain works: A high-density EEG study showing advantages of drawing over typing for learning. *Frontiers in Psychology*, *8*. https://doi.org/10.3389/fpsyg.2017.00706

9

Interacting with Technologies

Developing Digital Literacy Skills

Watching Eli swipe the screen of an iPad as easily as turning pages of a book caught me off guard at first. How could a toddler know how to work with this piece of technology so effortlessly? Swiping, clicking, and tapping seemed intuitive to Eli and almost like these actions were their own developing set of print concepts. These "digital print concepts" were emerging in Eli's repertoire of literacy behaviours relatively quickly once he was introduced to a touchscreen device. Although it seemed like he was instinctively developing these digital print concepts, there would have been modelling of these behaviours going on at home and out in the world. The first few apps Eli tried out included shape sorting, letter tracing, and drawing. Of course, all these activities could have been done using hands-on material, and he certainly did continue to make use of these materials just as he had been doing, but there seemed to be something new and interesting that Eli was drawn to when interacting with digital numeracy and literacy concepts.

As a parent, I would sometimes debate the idea of allowing Eli to use a touchscreen device, paying particular attention to the recommendations suggested by the different health organizations as well as the concerns of overuse and addiction that research has shown in adolescent and adult populations (Liu et al., 2022).

DOI: 10.4324/9781032688558-9

The American Academy of Paediatrics, for instance, cautions parents when selecting applications for their toddlers and children; they emphasize digital technologies and media should be carefully selected with high-quality content and developmentally appropriate, and should never replace a physical or social experience (2016). I eventually eased up on myself and the anxiety I was feeling when I considered all the various experiences exposed to Eli. I also kept a close eye on his behaviours before, during, and after his use of a touchscreen device. Based on my observations, he was still just as interested in books, drawing materials, and pretend play as he had always been. Our decision to include digital technologies in Eli's play and learning was an inherent one, and we made digital apps part of a balanced home literacy environment.

Defining digital literacy

We live in a world surrounded by digital technologies and multimedia, so it isn't surprising that digital and interactive multimedia seem ubiquitous in many homes, schools, and communities. *Digital literacy* is quite a broad term and has evolved over the last several decades. Definitions include the need for a variety of skills, such as skills involved in deciphering complex images and sounds, navigating networks and the internet, knowing about intended audience, and skills related to the use of digital tools (Lankshear & Knobel, 2008; Teichert, 2018; Yelland, 2018). Media Smarts (n.d.), an online hub for understanding and learning about digital and media literacies, defines *digital media literacy* as "the ability to critically, effectively and responsibly access, use, understand and engage with media of all kinds" (see Figure 9.1). It's about being an engaged and critical media user and building skills to access and navigate digital networks, analyse and evaluate media in a critical way, and use digital and media tools for creative and personal endeavours.

Rather than replacing Eli's experiences or learning opportunities, I started to view digital technologies as supplemental,

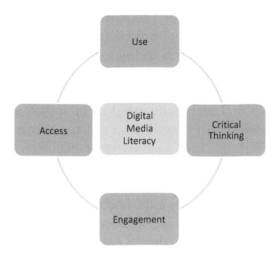

FIGURE 9.1 Digital media literacy.

complimenting and extending his literacy learning from more hands-on materials. As I read more and more about what is being said about screentime, I found some commonalities across various policies. The International Literacy Association summarizes these points in their position statement and research brief on digital resources in early childhood literacy development (2019, p. 3):

◆ Selection of high-quality digital media conveying content that supports curricular and learning goals and includes minimal distractors (e.g., ads, links that take users away from a site).
◆ Integration of digital technologies in ways that complement and enhance learning with other essential materials and activities.
◆ Use of technology that supports development of creativity, exploration, collaboration, problem-solving, and knowledge development.
◆ Use of technology to strengthen home-school connections.
◆ Access to assistive technologies to support equitable opportunities for learning.

Overall, the International Literacy Association suggests:

> Careful, intentional, and developmentally appropriate use of digital texts and tools can build young children's language and literacy skills while providing young children with opportunities to deepen their understanding about the forms and functions of digital texts in meaning making.
>
> (2019, p. 2)

Indeed, when incorporated into a literacy environment with balance, appropriateness, and quality in mind, the use of digital technology can have a meaningful and positive effect on children's growth in language and literacy, and does prepare children for living and learning in a digital world. When apps are selected for their high-quality literacy content and focussed activities such as letter matching, tracing letters, and forming letters, there is the potential to foster alphabet skills, early writing, and both non-digital and digital print concepts. For instance, children ages two to five who were introduced to literacy-related activities on a tablet during an experimental study showed significantly higher scores at post-test in letter knowledge, print concepts, and name writing than children who engaged in the literacy activities without any technology (Neumann, 2018). Of course, this is just one study, and the context and type of activities certainly need to be taken into consideration when interpreting the results. The author, however, does note that the findings showed how tablets can positively support letter name and sound learning. With that said, how parents and early years teachers can best use digital tools at home and in the classroom to support early literacy requires further investigation (Neumann, 2018).

Guidelines for parents and teachers

Below is a list of guidelines for parents and practitioners looking to incorporate digital technologies into their child's learning.

It's based on the International Literacy Association's review of the literature and considers the quality of the digital resources, opportunities for engagement, and connections to non-digital resources as well as home-school connections (2019).

1. Review and select high-quality digital resources that afford opportunities not otherwise provided by traditional resources, convey accurate content, contain few, if any, features that distract from the content, contain no advertisements, and support creativity, imagination, and collaboration.
2. Provide meaningful opportunities for engagement and learning with and through digital technologies by encouraging collaborative digital experiences and being present with children as they play.
3. Blend use of digital and non-digital resources by ensuring that you retain the use of printed books and writing materials.
4. For educators, build home-school connections by learning about tools parents are using with their children at home.

Multimodal and multimedia learning

The multimodal aspect of digital literacy is certainly one advantage of incorporating digital technologies into your home or classroom environment (ILA, 2019). *Multimodal* denotes the many ways meaning-making is embodied and expressed in our everyday communication (Teichert & Salman, 2021). When information is delivered through more than one mode, research has shown that learning can be enhanced (Chiou et al., 2015; Kennedy et al., 2013; Mayer, 2014). Technology can often provide a multimodal or multimedia environment; during multimodal and multimedia learning, knowledge is constructed from words (spoken or printed) and pictures (graphics, illustrations, videos). In multimedia learning, individuals can often learn more deeply from the combination of words and pictures than from words alone;

individuals do this by constructing a coherent mental representation from the presented material (Mayer, 2014; Schnotz, 2014). The addition of interesting but irrelevant material, however, can also distract the learner, who, because of the irrelevant "distractor," could become less engaged with the more relevant material (Scheiter & Eitel, 2017). Digital literacy can incorporate multiple modes or formats of information and, as I mentioned earlier, involves skills in deciphering complex images and sounds, operational skills or digital print concepts, and the ability to recognize the intended audience as well as the author's intent (Teichert & Salman, 2021). Multimodal features of touchscreen devices, like sounds, animations, and text, can certainly engage children's attention in multisensory ways by stimulating visual, auditory, kinaesthetic, and tactile senses (Roskos et al., 2014).

Digital technologies in early years environments

After reviewing existing research studies on age-appropriate uses of digital technology in preschool and kindergarten classes, Teichert and Salman (2021) suggest ways in which tablets and interactive technologies can be incorporated into early years environments. They suggest various opportunities for social collaboration and creativity and discuss how tablets can provide inclusive opportunities for children learning English as an additional language and even narrow the digital divide, where children who otherwise cannot access digital technology can have the opportunity to develop digital literacy skills.

Mantilla and Edwards (2019) also provide us with four considerations for the appropriate use of digital technologies in the early years: healthy practices, relationships, pedagogy, and digital play (see Figure 9.2).

Healthy practices include modelling and encouraging correct posture, encouraging short bursts of seated digital technology use broken by activities involving whole-body movement, encouraging video-chat with toddlers that incorporates live interactions, and fostering toddler fine motor development with active use of touchscreen technologies (Mantilla & Edwards,

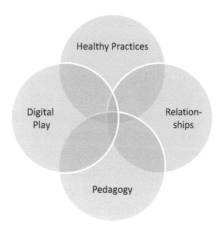

FIGURE 9.2 Considerations for the use of digital technologies in the early years.

2019). Second, Mantilla and Edwards (2019) suggest building in time to engage in the technology with your children, whether at home or in a classroom environment. Enhanced learning from digital technologies can occur with increased parent-child or adult-child interactions (Mantilla & Edwards, 2019). Just as you might support your child's oral language development and comprehension through a shared book reading activity, share ideas and ask questions around the digital activity in which the child is engaged. In terms of pedagogy, Mantilla and Edwards (2019) recommend parents and educators relate the use of digital technologies to children's interests and already existing activities, and foster collaboration where children work in pairs or small groups during digital technology use. Finally, the idea of digital play can range from exploratory to more directive types of play using digital technologies. For instance, preschool and kindergarten children can use a touchscreen device and slow-motion software to take photographs, create animations, and narrate and create movies (Fleer, 2017).

Acquiring digital literacy skills has also been linked to skills in STEAM—Science, Technology, Engineering, Arts, and Math. Skills in STEAM expand technical, scientific, critical, and creative thinking and also promote cognitive skills including problem-solving, working memory, and self-regulation (Siekmann & Korbel, 2016). These are skills that transcend STEAM and are important in our everyday interactions with the world around us. While it is critically important to consider the recommendations and guidelines around screentime use and how to best incorporate digital technologies into children's learning, being a positive digital citizen starts with supporting our youngest learners as they begin to navigate their digital world.

Tips for supporting the development of digital literacy at home and in the classroom

♦ Consider the quality of apps and other digital tools.
♦ Incorporate digital tools with multimedia that enhances learning; try to minimize distractors.
♦ Encourage collaboration and be present during your child's digital play; co-create!
♦ Encourage and model healthy practices.
♦ Balance digital literacy with non-digital literacy activities.

Recommended literacy apps for toddlers, preschoolers, and kindergarteners

♦ *ABCmouse—Early Learning Academy*
♦ *Bob Books Reading Magic #1*
♦ *Epic!-Kids' Books and Videos*
♦ *iMovie*
♦ *iWriteWords*
♦ *Lexia Core5 Reading*
♦ *Montessori Words and Phonics*
♦ *Starfall ABCs*
♦ *Starfall Learn to Read*
♦ *Storyline Online*

References

Chiou, C.C., Tien, L.C., & Lee, L.T. (2015). Effects on learning of multimedia animation combined with multidimensional concept maps. *Computers & Education, 80*, 211–223. https://doi.org/10.1016/j.compedu.2014.09.002

Fleer, M. (2017). Digital role-play: The changing conditions of children's play in preschool settings. *Mind, Culture, and Activity, 24*(1), 3–17. doi: 10.1080/10749039.2016.1247456

International Literacy Association. (2019). *Digital resources in early childhood literacy development [Position statement and research brief].* Newark, DE: Author.

Kennedy, M.J., Driver, M.K., Pullen, P.C., Ely, E., & Cole, M.T. (2013). Improving teacher candidates' knowledge of phonological awareness: A multimedia approach. *Computers & Education, 64,* 42–51. http://dx.doi.org/10.1016/j.compedu.2013.01.010

Lankshear, C., & Knobel, M. (2008). *Digital literacies: Concepts, policies and practices.* Peter Lang.

Liu, J., Riesch, S., Tien, J., Lipman, T., Pinto-Martin, J., & O'Sullivan, A. (2022). Screen media overuse and associated physical, cognitive, and emotional/behavioral outcomes in children and adolescents: An integrative review. *Journal of Pediatric Health Care, 36*(2), 99–109. https://doi.org/10.1016/j.pedhc.2021.06.003

Mantilla, A., & Edwards, S. (2019). Digital technology use by and with young children: A systematic review for the statement on young children and digital technologies. *Australasian Journal of Early Childhood, 44*(2), 182–195. doi:10.1177/1836939119832744

Mayer, R.E. (2014). Incorporating motivation into multimedia learning. *Learning and Instruction, 29,* 171–173. https://doi.org/10.1016/j.learninstruc.2013.04.003

Neumann, M.M. (2018). Using tablets and apps to enhance emergent literacy skills in young children. *Early Childhood Research Quarterly, 42,* 239–246. http://dx.doi.org/10.1016/j.ecresq.2017.10.006

Roskos, K., Burstein, K., Shang, Y., & Gray, E. (2014). Young children's engagement with e-books at school: Does device matter? *Sage Open, 4*(1). https://doi.org/10.1177/2158244013517244.

Scheiter, K., & Eitel, A. (2017). The use of eye tracking as a research and instructional tool in multimedia learning. In C. Was, F. Sansosti, & B. Morris (Eds.), *Eye-tracking technology applications in educational research* (pp. 143–165). Hershey, PA: IGI Global.

Schnotz, W. (2014). Integrated model of text and picture comprehension. In R.E. Mayer (Ed.), *Cambridge handbook of multimedia learning* (2nd ed., pp. 72–103). Cambridge, England: Cambridge University Press.

Siekmann, G., & Korbel, K. (2016). Defining 'STEM' skills: Review and synthesis of the literature. *National Centre for Vocational Education Research*. https://files.eric.ed.gov/fulltext/ED570655.pdf

Teichert, L. (2018). *An examination of young children's digital literacy practices in the home before and during the transition to kindergarten* [Unpublished doctoral dissertation]. University of British Columbia.

Teichert, L., & Salman, M. (2021). Digital technology in the early years: A reflection. *McGill Journal of Education/Revue des sciences de l'éducation de McGill*, *56*(2/3). https://id.erudit.org/iderudit/1096456ar

Yelland, N.J. (2018). A pedagogy of multiliteracies: Young children and multimodal learning with tablets. *British Journal of Educational Technology*, *49*(5), 847–858. https://doi.org/10.1111/bjet.12635

10

Reading in Cars

Motivation for Literacy

During Eli's first two years of life, he seemed to do well traveling in a car. By the time Eli turned one, we had done a few relatively long road trips and, for the most part, he'd been quite a trouper. While on route to our various destinations, Eli would peruse his board books like he did at home, only in the car he'd also be balancing the books on his lap in his car seat. On one of our ventures out east, I glanced over at Eli "reading" a book about an Easter egg hunt. As he stared at the different images and flipped through the pages, I started to reflect on how and when someone begins to read for pleasure. What motivates someone, regardless of their age, to pick up a book, whether it's in a car or at home, and read?

Motivation for reading and engagement in literacy has been well researched over the past few decades (Guthrie & Coddington, 2009; Guthrie & Klauda, 2015; Nevo & Vaknin-Nusbaum, 2020; Wigfield & Guthrie, 2013). And if you are or were a classroom teacher, then you're likely nodding your head yes, motivation matters. We read for enjoyment and stay engaged in reading because we're interested, we're curious. Interest often drives someone to learn more about a subject or stay entertained by a topic. Or if you're like me, you discover an author who has a certain writing style that catches your attention, and you spend all your free time reading every book they've ever written

DOI: 10.4324/9781032688558-10

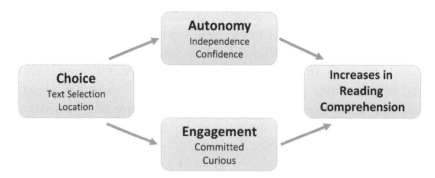

FIGURE 10.1 Benefits of choice in text selection.

(it's so satisfying). Any teacher can likely point out an engaged reader—someone who spends long stretches of time reading, is focused and concentrating, picks up a book in the car, at home, or in a cozy book nook at school, and often wants to tell you all about what they've just read. They're also given a choice about what to read; choice is certainly a driving force, a motivator, and as Figure 10.1 shows, has been linked to greater autonomy, higher engagement levels, and better comprehension (Guthrie & Klauda, 2015).

I like how reading researchers John Guthrie and Allen Wigfield put it: "An engaged reader comprehends a text not only because she can do it, but because she is motivated to do it" (2000, p. 404). Of course, an engaged reader must possess the basic skills of reading, including alphabet knowledge and decoding skills, and attaining these skills can be motivating in itself. However, do the basics always need to come first before someone becomes interested in books and feels motivated to read? Probably not, as any kindergartener ready to listen to Robert Munsch read aloud *The Paper Bag Princess* would tell you (1980).

Motivation versus engagement

Motivation for literacy can indeed be viewed as a foundational element of reading and certainly deserves recognition as being at least a significant contributor to learning to read and reading engagement. Motivation differs from engagement in that the former term refers to an individual's personal goals, values, and beliefs with respect to the topics, processes, and outcomes of literacy (Guthrie & Wigfield, 2000). Engagement, on the other hand, refers to an individual's actual involvement in an activity, like reading, and is usually reflected in behaviour, affect, and cognition (Guthrie & Wigfield, 2000). Figure 10.2 presents a visual representation of the relationship between motivation for and engagement in literacy.

Both motivation and engagement are reciprocally related, where an increase in one will likely increase the other. But motivation for reading has also been suggested to be a foundational process for reading engagement; it's what activates someone's behaivours and engagement in reading in the first place (Guthrie & Wigfield, 2000). Extrinsic and intrinsic motivation, self-efficacy, and choice are factors that affect someone's motivation to read. Before delving into each of these constructs, let's start with an example, a time when you felt *unmotivated* to read and how that might have affected your level of engagement and, ultimately, text comprehension.

Consider a time when you've felt unmotivated to read a particular text: perhaps in high school you were given a task to read a chapter from a text on a topic in which you had little interest. Halfway through the third page of the chapter, you realize that you haven't retained any information that you have supposedly just read. You may have read the words, but at some point, your mind wandered off and you started thinking about an unrelated topic. Realizing this major omission, you flip back to the start of the chapter and begin again, perhaps this time with accompanying self-talk to help you get started. The lack of engagement

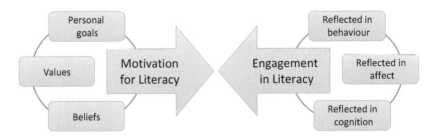

FIGURE 10.2 Motivation for and engagement in literacy.

in reading this chapter is likely because you aren't motivated to read it—the chapter doesn't interest you; it was assigned to you rather than a book that you chose to read; and you're not even sure of the usefulness of the information. One aspect that could help you sustain your attention is that the chapter was assigned for a course you're taking, and you want to do well in the course. Although coming from an external source, this pressure to do well might contribute to your motivation to read the chapter and even maintain engagement with the material.

This is *extrinsic motivation*, which relates to the desire to receive external recognition, rewards, or incentives as a result of, in this case, reading a selected text (Deci & Ryan, 2008). Although seen as more surface-level strategies for encouraging reading, recognition, rewards, and incentives do not necessarily have a negative impact an individual's motivation for reading. Attempting to reach a goal of reading 100 books over the summer break or getting through an assigned chapter because you have the desire to do well in the course can certainly be incentives to become engaged in reading. These types of external motivators also have the potential to lead to a more internalized motivation. Even though a good grade was an initial motivating factor, there might be a piece of information that catches your attention and interests you, which might, in turn, increase your internal enjoyment for reading about the given topic.

While extrinsic motivation refers to external sources, *intrinsic motivation* refers to an individual's enjoyment and interest in activities, like reading; the activity is performed for its own sake (Deci & Ryan, 1985, 2008). Motivation researchers suggest that intrinsically motivated activities have an experimental component, which can spark excitement, interest, and enjoyment in the activity (Deci & Ryan, 1985, 2008; Guthrie & Wigfield, 2000). In terms of literacy and reading motivation, the spark of excitement is combined with a curiosity to learn about and understand a topic of interest. You might be intrinsically motivated to read a non-fiction text about a historical event because you are genuinely interested in learning more about the subject; you find reading about historical events enjoyable and are inherently satisfied during and after picking up a historical text.

Self-efficacy for reading

Self-efficacy is another aspect of reading motivation. Generally, *self-efficacy* can be described as someone's judgement of their own capabilities in and performances on a particular task (Bandura, 1977, 1997). Children with high self-efficacy for reading will more likely see difficult reading tasks as challenging and work diligently to master them; they will persist even when they are confronted with unfamiliar words or difficult content (Schunk & Zimmerman, 1997). Children with low self-efficacy for reading, on the other hand, would likely avoid challenging books or books altogether; children with low self-efficacy for reading don't necessarily see themselves as readers and will be more likely to give up when faced with adversity (Guthrie & Wigfield, 2000).

There is a strong correlation between self-efficacy and intrinsic motivation; children with high self-efficacy to read are more likely to be intrinsically motivated to read and vice versa (Wigfield & Cambria, 2010). A child with high intrinsic motivation and high self-efficacy is, as you may have guessed, more likely to be an active reader (Guthrie & Wigfield, 2000). Unfortunately, research in reading motivation has shown that a shift often occurs around the fourth-grade level where children's reading motivation is more likely to decline during this time (Guthrie & Wigfield, 2000). There are several possibilities for this decline, including a decrease in self-efficacy, greater awareness of their performance, and less opportunities to select texts of personal interest (Barber & Klauda, 2020). The decline is also influenced by how well children have done on similar activities and the feedback and encouragement they receive from others (Guthrie & Wigfield, 2000). Given the fact that reading experiences, whether positive or negative, can have an enormous impact on a child's self-efficacy and overall reading motivation, it's important to consider your role, as the parent or teacher, on your child's self-efficacy for reading. Researchers suggest that it's not enough to teach children the basic skills of reading, we must also teach our children to want to read (Brandt et al., 2021; Gambrell, 2015). Fostering motivation for reading starts with cultivating a safe space for reading to be practised and enjoyed.

Simple actions to nurture motivation for reading

Nurturing children's motivation for reading can happen through relatively simple actions at home and in the classroom. Choice, time, and diversity are three key components to consider when fostering reading motivation. Let's start with choice.

Choice

Provide *choice* in reading, whether through text topics, text types, or reading location. Choice is widely acknowledged as a factor that can affect an individual's motivation to read and even enhance it (Guthrie & Wigfield, 2000). When children are given a choice in what they read and where to read, even if it's a choice from just two given options, their interest in the activity of reading, their engagement, increases. Fostering choice might seem like an obvious motivator and can indeed be a game-changer. You can promote choice by finding books that your child or students are interested in reading. These should be both fiction and non-fiction and include a variety of text types. The goal is to use your child's or students' interests as a launching point for reading. Take this idea even further and have your child or students create wish lists and have a say in the books that they would like to read. Regular library or bookstore visits can be a great first step (and a healthy habit) to instigate a love for reading.

Time

Create *time* for reading and talking about books. The research on silent reading in classrooms is mixed; however, there are benefits of allowing children to read to themselves, especially those with high levels of self-efficacy and intrinsic motivation (Merke et al., 2023). Silently reading to yourself can have a direct effect on sustained reading engagement, especially if there are additional elements connected to the silent reading time, like student accountability that might involve note-taking or a reading log (Merke et al., 2023). For those children who have low self-efficacies, lack intrinsic motivation, and require instruction in basic decoding skills, time in the classroom is likely better used to foster decoding skills, particularly with more challenging texts. Time for independent reading is still needed and can indeed allow a child to become interested in a topic they've selected. This is where the importance of varied text types, including digital texts, come into play. For children who require instruction in decoding and fluency, provide them with the option to read a digital or audio book or a graphic novel so they too can build their enjoyment in reading for pleasure. Graphic novels are like comic books and usually include vivid illustrations and limited text. They can be a window into reading for reluctant readers.

When discussing books with your child or students provide them with sentence starters to prompt their thinking. Prompts might include:

- ◆ I was thinking that the main character…
- ◆ My favourite part of the book was…
- ◆ I felt *happy/sad/curious* when…
- ◆ It was interesting how…
- ◆ An interesting fact I read about is…
- ◆ When I read about … I was reminded of a time when…
- ◆ I wonder…

Diverse texts

A final, but particularly important, consideration is to ensure that children see themselves in the books they are reading by including *diverse texts* in your home or classroom library. Books need to reflect your child and students' cultures and family experiences; diverse books give children a window into the diverse world in which we live, expose children to a wide range of books, and help build empathy and background knowledge (Flores & Osorio, 2021). This concept can be thought of as "mirrors and windows" and was first introduced by Rudine Sims Bishop in her iconic essay *Mirrors, windows, and sliding glass doors* (1990). Books, Bishop describes, are sometimes windows, "offering views of worlds that may be real or imagined, familiar or strange" (1990). A window can also be a mirror and in the mirror's reflection "we can see our own lives and experiences as part of the larger human experience" (1990). Mirror books can reflect different aspects of our identity, including family, gender, race, ethnicity, culture, and language (Flores & Osorio, 2021). Including mirror books in your home or classroom library allows children to validate or affirm their identities, share their stories, and show others of possibilities of who and what they can be (Flores & Osorio, 2021). Window books provide children with opportunities to see aspects of a world that are different than their own (Flores & Osorio, 2021). They can introduce readers to new perspectives, allow readers to develop new interests, and engage readers with important topics and social issues (Flores & Osorio, 2021).

From the field: Fostering motivation for reading

During my school visits I was curious to not only learn about how reading was taught, but also how the teachers motivated their students to read. What did reading for pleasure look like in these school contexts? What types of reading activities were especially effective in supporting students' motivation for reading? How did the educators foster motivation for reading? These were a few of the questions I pondered when I stepped into schools and spoke to classroom teachers. What was common across contexts was a love for literacy. Supporting children's motivation for reading was at the core of my conversations and discussed in a way that intertwined other aspects of literacy, like oral language, alphabet knowledge, and vocabulary development (Beach, 2024). Relationship building was also mentioned in several conversations. A Montessori teacher, for instance, described how the children's interests lie in the teachers' relationships with the children; the children need to "know that they're loved, and their voices are heard." Choice is a large component of a child's day-to-day literacy learning in a Montessori classroom, helping to build the child's autonomy, independence, and self-confidence. Choice in text selection, however, goes hand-in-hand with providing children with the tools for success.

Another Montessori teacher described how children must be taught the skills in decoding and comprehending text to really enjoy reading and the process of selecting texts to read for pleasure.

As parents and teachers, we want to instil a love for literacy in our children, whether it's our children at home or in the classroom. Start with creating a safe and comfortable environment to read with and to your children. From there, provide choice, encourage discussions, and surround your children with a variety of texts. Setting up the habit of reading from an early age can indeed foster a love for reading and lifelong learning. Simple activities can have a transformative impact on a child's decision to pick up a book, whether in the car or at home, and read.

Tips for supporting motivation for reading

◆ Provide children with choice, time, and a variety of texts.
◆ Make regular visits to the school or local library.
◆ Include diverse texts in your home or classroom library.
◆ Ensure that books in your home or classroom library match the children's interests.
◆ Provide children with the option to listen to audio books and read graphic novels and non-fiction texts.

Recommended graphic novels

Ages 3–6

◆ *Awesome Dawson* by Chris Gall
◆ *Blinky the Spacecat* by Ashley Spires
◆ *Dear Fish* by Chris Gall
◆ *Jack and the Box* by Art Spiegelman
◆ *The Adventures of Polo* by Regix Faller

Ages 6–9

◆ *Babymouse #4: Rock Star* by Matthew Holm and Jennifer L. Holm (from the Babymouse series)

- *Bone: Eyes of the Storm* by Jeff Smith
- *El Deafo* by Cece Bell
- *Owly: Flying Lessons* by Andy Runton
- *Sardine in Outer Space* by Emmanuel Guibert, Illustrator: Joann Sfar

References

Bandura, A. (1977). Self-efficacy: Toward a unifying theory of behavioral change. *Psychological Review*, *84*(2), 191–215.

Bandura, A. (1997). *Self-efficacy: The exercise of control.* W.H. Freeman.

Barber, A.T., & Klauda, S.L. (2020). How reading motivation and engagement enable reading achievement: Policy implications. *Policy Insights from the Behavioral and Brain Sciences*, *7*(1), 27–34.

Beach, P. (2024). Literacy in Montessori schools: Perspectives from Canada, Mexico, and Italy. *Annual Conference of the American Educational Research Association.*

Bishop, R.S. (1990). *Mirrors, windows, and sliding glass doors. Perspectives*, *6*(3), ix–xi.

Brandt, L., Sharp, A.C., & Gardner, D.S. (2021). Examination of teacher practices on student motivation for reading. *The Reading Teacher*, *74*(6), 723–731. https://doi.org/10.1002/trt.1999

Deci, E.L., & Ryan, R.M. (1985). *Intrinsic motivation and self-determination in human behavior.* Plenum.

Deci, E.L., & Ryan, R.M. (2008). Facilitating optimal motivation and psychological well-being across life's domains. *Canadian Psychology*, *49*, 14–23. https://doi.org/10.1037/0708-5591.49.1.14

Flores, T., & Osorio, S. (2021). *Why diverse books matter: Mirrors and Windows.* Colorín Colorado. https://www.colorincolorado.org/article/why-diverse-books-matter-mirrors-and-windows

Gambrell, L.B. (2015). Getting students hooked on the reading habit. *The Reading Teacher*, *69*(3), 259–263. https://doi.org/10.1002/trtr.1423

Guthrie, J.T., & Coddington, C.S. (2009). Reading motivation. In K. R. Wentzel & D. B. Miele (Eds.), *Handbook of motivation at school* (pp. 517–540). Routledge. https://doi.org/10.4324/9780203879498

Guthrie, J.T., & Klauda, S.L. (2015). Engagement and motivational processes in reading. In *Handbook of individual differences in reading*
(pp. 41–53). Routledge.

Guthrie, J. & Wigfield, A. (2000). Engagement and motivation in reading.
In M.L. Kimil, P.B. Mosenthal, P.D. Pearson, & R. Barr (Eds.), *Handbook
of reading research* (pp. 403–422). Routledge.

Merke, S., Ganushchak, L., & van Steensel, R. (2023). Effects of additions to
independent silent reading on students' reading proficiency, motivation, and behavior: Results of a meta-analysis. *Educational Research
Review*, 100572. https://doi.org/10.1016/j.edurev.2023.100572

Munsch, R. (1980). *The paper bag princess*. Annick Press.

Nevo, E., & Vaknin-Nusbaum, V. (2020). Enhancing motivation to read and
reading abilities in first grade. *Educational Psychology*, *40*(1), 22–41.

Schunk, D.H., & Zimmerman, B.J. (1997). Developing self-efficacious
readers and writers: The role of social and self-regulatory processes.
In J.T. Guthrie & A. Wigfield (Eds.), *Reading engagement: Motivating
readers through integrated instruction* (pp. 43–50). International Reading Association.

Wigfield, A., & Cambria, J. (2010). Students' achievement values, goal ori-
entations, and interest: Definitions, development, and relations to
achievement outcomes. *Developmental Review*, *30*(1), 1–35. https://
doi.org/10.1016/j.dr.2009.12.001

Wigfield, A., & Guthrie, J.T. (2013). Motivation for reading: An overview.
*Motivation for Reading: Individual, Home, Textual, and Classroom
Perspectives*, 57–58.

For Product Safety Concerns and Information please contact our
EU representative GPSR@taylorandfrancis.com Taylor & Francis
Verlag GmbH, Kaufingerstraße 24, 80331 München, Germany